A BAYOU BAR

The Louisiana State Bar Association

1804–1941

A BAYOU BAR

THE LOUISIANA STATE BAR ASSOCIATION 1804–1941

BY WARREN M. BILLINGS

UNIVERSITY OF NEW ORLEANS PRESS

A Bayou Bar: The Louisiana State Bar Association, 1804-1941

ISBN: 9781608013012

First edition
Printed in the United States of America on acid-free paper.

University of New Orleans Press
2000 Lakeshore Drive
New Orleans, Louisiana 70148
unopress.org

Cover and interior design by Kevin Stone

For T. Gregory Schafer

CONTENTS

ACKNOWLEDGEMENTS

My friend, former student, and co-author Mark F. Fernandez and Patricia Carlin O'Keefe, distinguished professor of history at Loyola University in New Orleans, gave thoughtful advice at an early stage in the book's gestation.

Another of my former students, Louisiana library historian Florence M. Jumonville, shared her immense knowledge of nineteenth-century private libraries.

Thanks are due to four law librarian colleagues. At the Law Library of Louisiana, Miriam Childs, Tara Cunningham, and Cynthia Jones tracked down citations to original materials and, where possible, provided digital copies. Director James E. Duggan arranged access to digital collections at the Tulane Law Library and provided digital copies of many items.

Georgia Chadwick, retired law librarian of Louisiana, merits special notice. Throughout the project, she rummaged databases that were inaccessible to me and found many choice items that I would have missed. Her connections to Tulane University, the Land Records Divisions of Orleans Parish, and the New Orleans Public Library produced results that were invaluable too. She read iterations of the manuscript and caught inaccuracies that would have diminished the finished book.

Mary Sarah Bilder, founders professor of law at the Boston College of Law; E. Phelps Gay, former president of the Louisiana State Bar Association; and James F. Sefcik, former director of the Louisiana State Museum also read the manuscript and offered incisive comments. I thank them for that.

Acknowledgments are due Frazar Memorial Library at McNeese State University, The Historic New Orleans Collection, Northwest Louisiana Archives at Louisiana State University Shreveport, and the Supreme Court of Louisiana for furnishing the digital images that appear throughout the book and for their gracious permission to publish them.

As with all my previous writings, Carol D. Billings was a constant inspiration.

This book is for my son-in-law, attorney T. Gregory Schafer.

Preface

This is a book about bar associations and their place in national life. In one form or another those organizations existed even before the beginning of the Republic, and the number of them grew throughout the nineteenth and twentieth centuries. Each arose from distinctive circumstances that typified legal patterns that were not only unique to a particular state but were also common to the American legal profession as a whole. Their influence with state legislatures, courts, and law schools fixed standards of legal education and controlled the practice of law. Many began as private societies that attracted small, highly selective, self-perpetuating memberships but slowly evolved into state-wide associations to which all lawyers belonged. Their stories have seldom caught the scholarly eye. Because they have not, I reasoned that a book about the Louisiana State Bar Association from 1804 to 1941 could be taken as illustrative of how such entities came to be.

Readers may wonder why an historian of early Virginia chose to write such a book. The answer is a plain one. I was reared in the Old Dominion where I was attracted to professing history as a calling but I have spent most of my career at the University of New Orleans. Like other emigrants, I knew little about Louisiana, except that it was "different" from other parts of the country. At first appreciating those differences was of no interest because I was about the business of trying to understand colonial Virginians and their legal culture. However, I was enticed to Louisiana law as I got to know the late Albert Tate, Jr., a justice of the Supreme Court of Louisiana, and discovered that we shared a common interest in the history of law and the value of judicial records for historical enquiry. Those early encounters blossomed into an enduring friendship that eventually resulted in our drawing up an arrangement whereby the University of New Orleans became the repository of the Louisiana Supreme Court's archives for the years between 1813 and 1921. I planned to go no farther than assisting with the deposit because I really knew nothing about the court or Louisiana law. My attitude changed after I started encouraging my graduate students to use the records as a source of seminar exercises, conference papers, and theses. Judge Tate and his colleagues also pressed me to study the court, which led to my appointment as its official historian. The more I delved into the collection the more the court and aspects of its existence intrigued me and led to my being an architect of the New Louisiana Legal History. All the while my Virginia work took precedence until the publication of my most recent book *Statute Law In Colonial Virginia: Governors, Assemblymen, Revisals, And The Forging Of The Old Dominion*. After it went to press in 2020, I decided the time had come to write a book that was connected to my Louisiana interests.

* * *

In one form or another the Louisiana State Bar Association (LSBA) has existed for more than two centuries as it passed from an elite, highly selective congregation of lawyers to a mandatory association. Its earliest origins date to interchanges between legislators, jurists, and lawyers that commenced with the congressional organization of the Territory of Orleans. Before statehood, the Superior Court for the Territory of Orleans looked to attorneys for help in drafting its processes and screening prospective lawyers. After statehood supreme court judges relied on certain well-placed New Orleans lawyers for help in fashioning their rules of practice and standards for their supervision of the bar, and in time they encouraged the founding of the New Orleans Law Association (NOLA).

Chartered under state law as a private charitable corporation, the incorporators established it as a members-only library and sought to enhance the reputation of Crescent City attorneys. It aided the justices with their administrative tasks, it recommended would-be attorneys, it assisted in opening the forerunner of the Tulane University School of Law, and its members were highly visible in state and local politics. Throughout the Civil War members fought for the Confederacy and died as traitors. Reduced to a shadow, the NOLA recovered slowly during Reconstruction. It attracted former Confederates and others, all of whom were steeped in unyielding White supremacy and pernicious myths of the Lost Cause that held fast deep into the twentieth century, and even now they have yet to be entirely erased from memory.

Rechartered in 1899 as the Louisiana Bar Association (LBA), the organization retained its corporate status and close ties to the Supreme Court. Its leaders strove to grow its law library and its membership. As its presence extended statewide so did its influence with the General Assembly, the courts, and the law schools at Tulane, Louisiana State, and Loyola universities. It renamed itself the LSBA in 1929. By that year, the association's vision of Louisiana contrasted starkly with the views of the radical populist Huey P. Long and his followers. Holding to that vision nearly destroyed the LSBA after it lost its fierce fight with Long over an election to the Louisiana Supreme Court. Long and his minions had their revenge. They enacted a rival statutory, state-governed bar association to which all lawyers were required to belong, and they limited the court's authority over its rules. The LSBA hung on until lawyers successfully lobbied Governor Sam H. Jones, the General Assembly, and the Louisiana Supreme Court to reconstitute it as a mandatory statewide society in 1941.

All of this caught my fancy and inspired questions. How did it happen? Who made history? What was the connection between the Louisiana Supreme Court and New Orleans? Who started the New Orleans Law Association? How did it become the state bar association? How was it nearly destroyed? And how was it resurrected into the modern organization?

Turning to the extant documentary record, I sought answers to these questions that I assembled into the book that follows. But like broken crockery significant parts of that record are beyond recovery, and their loss limits the narrative. Memoirs, journals, and diaries are scarce. Survivors are often frustratingly vague or utterly useless. Letters and private papers are equally rare and unrevealing. The Supreme Court's own archives for the New Orleans sessions: minute books, docket books, opinion books, and case files are abundant and generally well preserved. On the other hand, virtually the entire archive for the Western Supreme Court sessions went missing in the nineteenth century. Acts of the General Assembly, reported cases argued in the Supreme Court, newspapers, magazines, and other contemporary printed works fill some of the holes. Other empty spaces are possible to plug only by conjecture. (There are more of those voids than I anticipated, and my inability to reduce their frequency is the book's greatest shortcoming.)

The book is developed in six chapters of varying length and detail. Chapter One is contextual. It lays out the passage of Louisiana from territory to state and focuses on the rise of the legal profession and its link to the Supreme Court. It explains the growing inability of the court to meet its responsibilities, and it describes how the court was reinvented by the Constitution of 1845. Leading figures are identified, and their roles are discussed. Chapter Two accounts for the founding of the NOLA and its transition from a society of like-minded city attorneys to a state-chartered charitable corporation. The founders and the incorporators are introduced, and their relations with the Louisiana Supreme Court are considered. (It is the shortest and most speculative chapter for reasons that become apparent as it unfolds.) How the NOLA fared from the Civil War through Reconstruction to its rechartering in 1899 as the LBA is the subject of Chapter Three. It tells how the war reduced the membership and how Union occupation of New Orleans shut it down for nearly a decade, after which it slowly recovered, drew close to the Supreme Court once more, and became firmly committed to Jim Crow. Chapter Four covers the years between 1899 and the 1930s. Attention is given to its expansion, its renaming as the LSBA, and its first clashes with Huey P. Long. Chapter Five recounts an action-packed fight with the Long organization over the election of John B. Fournet to the Supreme Court and its disastrous consequences for the LSBA. The final chapter describes the dynamics that fostered the creation of the modern bar in 1941. An epilogue concludes the book.

* * *

Readers who are familiar with my earlier essays about the Supreme Court will observe likenesses between them and parts of this book. Those were articles where I first considered issues that I take up here at length. Some were what might be called "idea pieces" whereas others were in the nature of reports on an individual or an episode from Louisiana's legal past. They were constrained by the confines of the article as a vehicle of printed communication and by what I did not know when I wrote them. They were never intended as preludes to book chapters. However, where pertinent, I have made full use of their content.

* * *

The Covid-19 pandemic confined me to my study while I assembled the book. That was not as much of an impediment as I first feared it might be. For starters, my library contains substantial holdings in early Louisiana legal titles. I still had all the research notes that I collected about the Supreme Court over the years, and I could draw on my earlier writings. That was enough to rough out an outline and to identify things that required new or deeper research. Then it was a question of how to do that research from my desk at home. The answer lay in an alternate universe of virtual reality that substitutes for the physical materials themselves. Digital aggregations the American Memory Project, Find A Grave, Google Books, HeinOnline, HathiTrust, JSTOR, Louisiana Digital Library, Project Muse, ProQuest, *64 Parishes Encyclopedia Online*, and Westlaw became instant hunting grounds at the stroke of a few keys on my iMac.

AUTHOR'S NOTE

First citations throughout the notes that are marked with a $_{\text{WB}}$ refer to items from my library. Unmarked first citations denote all other items that are curated in research and law libraries. Virtual copies are recorded in digital aggregations The Books Online Page, Google Books, and HathiTrust readily retrievable at the stroke of a few keys on a desktop computer or handheld device.

Biographies of leading figures derive from citations to the *Dictionary of Louisiana Biography Online*, the digital version of Glenn R. Conrad et al., eds., *A Dictionary of Louisiana Biography*, 3 vols. (Lafayette, La.: Louisiana Historical Association, 1988, 1998); the *American National Biography Online*, the digital version of John A. Garrity, et al., eds., *American National Biography*, 24 vols. (New York: Oxford University Press, 1999, 2000); or they derive from contemporary sources referred to in a particular biography.

Citations to the acts of the General Assembly are to the HeinOnline (Buffalo, NY,: William S. Hein & Company, 2000–) digital archive.

Citations to the items that document the dispute between Judge Thomas F. Porter and Attorney General E. A. Conway are to the Porter v. Conway case file (No. 33147) which is in the clerk's office at the Supreme Court in New Orleans.

Chapter One

Raising the Bar

In March 1804, Congress cleaved the Louisiana Purchase in two, and the smaller half, roughly the size of the modern Pelican State, became the Territory of Orleans. President Thomas Jefferson named his young cousin William Charles Cole Claiborne (1775–1817) governor and explicitly charged him to introduce American law but to allow the continuation of the *ancienne population*'s Hispano-Franco legal customs.[a] The result arose out of interchanges between jurists and lawyers; both started from the same point of reference: how to find a workable legal regime. Their quest yielded a blend of Anglo-American common law precepts and Hispano-Franco civilian principles that invested Louisiana with its distinctive mixed legal regime. Private law would be grounded largely upon civilian customs, criminal law would be based in common law habits, and the courts would be modeled on American usage. Early on, the Superior Court for the Territory of Orleans also looked to barristers for help in drafting its rules of practice and ways to screen prospective lawyers.[b]

When the authors wrote the Constitution of 1812, they provided for a hierarchical state judiciary that was patterned on an American model.[c] At the apex sat the Supreme Court of Louisiana that had "appellate jurisdiction only" in civil cases involving more than three hundred dollars.[d] It consisted of up to five judges, each of whom received an annual salary of five thousand dollars. They tried cases at New Orleans and in the town of Opelousas, the seat of a western appellate district, which comprised the remainder of the state (Morgan). However, the constitution said nothing about the Supreme Court's administrative powers or its relationship with lawyers, so the first General Assembly addressed those matters in the Judiciary Act of 1813.[1] The statute authorized three judges. They could "make and issue all mandates necessary for the exercise of [their] jurisdiction over the inferior tribunals," they could control their officers, and they could adopt any "needful rules" so long as their rules did not contravene the act or other state laws, and any rule changes required prior notice.[e] Another section of the act required the judges to test, license, and discipline anyone who wished to practice law. Without saying so, that authorization reflected a prevailing American assumption that deciding who should be lawyers and punishing any who misbehaved was best determined by higher court judges (La. § 17-18).

Explicit as the judiciary act seemed to be, it left the door open to a ponderable lack of clarity regarding its implementation. What mandates were necessary for the judges to exercise their jurisdiction over the courts below, and what was the nature of that authority? When it came to controlling officers of the Supreme Court, who were those individuals? Were they statutory officers or were they creations of the court? What rules of court were needful? And what standards applied to the regulation of anyone who practiced law in the state? Obviously, answers would come from the General Assembly and the judges, and they would change with experience over time, but immediately in 1812, the process began with the naming of the first court.[f] Governor Claiborne nominated Dominick Augustin Hall, George Mathews, and Pierre Derbigny to the state senate. The senators confirmed Hall and Mathews on February 22 and 23,

1 The state legislature is named the General Assembly of the State of Louisiana in the constitution (Morgan) although the now familiar "Legislature" has crept into usage.

1813 respectively, but they balked at Derbigny's nomination and refused to confirm him until March 9.

Hall (1765–1820) stands with those ghostly legal Louisianans whose influence on the Supreme Court and the profession was important but whose obscurity renders them all but forgotten. The little that may be said of him is told quickly. Hall was a South Carolinian who had a law practice in Charleston before President Jefferson put him on one of federal circuit courts. That circuit was abolished in 1802 so Jefferson sent him to the Territory of Orleans, where he became the preeminent federal trial judge in the American Southwest. After statehood, President James Madison nominated him to a newly created US district court in Louisiana. Hall resigned the seat and went to the Supreme Court but returned to the federal bench in July 1813. Notably, Hall was caught up in a fight for fining General Andrew Jackson, who ignored his writ of habeas corpus and jailed him.[g]

George Mathews (1774–1836) is somewhat better known. A Virginian, he was born in the frontier town of Staunton on the eve of the War for Independence. His father had been an officer in the Continental Army and a prisoner of war before he moved the family to Georgia, which he represented in Congress and was twice its governor. Young Mathews finished his education in Virginia. He returned to Georgia, read law, and became an attorney of considerable reputation. President Jefferson gave him a recess appointment to the territorial court in Mississippi, and when it lapsed in 1808, the president moved him to a seat on the Superior Court for the Territory of Orleans. Mathews came to his new post scarcely fluent in French or Spanish or in the civil law. He was a quick learner as he settled into his judicial duties and grew to be an able jurist who soon earned the respect of suitors, colleagues, and lawyers alike. His genial disposition, his command of American legal forms, and his jurisprudence more than qualified him in Governor Claiborne's calculations for a seat on the Supreme Court. He succeeded Hall as chief judge and presided until his death.[h]

George Mathews from the Louisiana Supreme Court Portrait Collection, Law Library of Louisiana, New Orleans.

Derbigny (1767–1829), was of noble parentage. He escaped revolutionary France and alighted in Saint Domingue before he lived with French refugees who found safe haven in and about Philadelphia. While in the City of Brotherly Love, he polished his mastery of English and American law, both of which were assets as he moved through Pittsburgh, the Illinois country, New Madrid, Florida, and Havana before he settled permanently in New Orleans in 1797. Rather quickly thereafter, he rose to prominence as a lawyer with a marked visibility in colonial and territorial politics. After the Louisiana Purchase, he was highly dubious of the intrusion of American law into Louisiana, and he staunchly advocated for immediate statehood, which set him opposite Governor Claiborne. Notwithstanding his stance, he earned places in the territorial legislative assembly and the state senate. Opposition did not prevent Claiborne from putting him on the Supreme Court, where he stayed until he resigned to run unsuccessfully for governor. Thomas Bolling Robertson won that election and chose Derbigny for his secretary of state, and he was also one of the architects of the Civil Code of 1825. He remained in the secretary's office until his own election as governor in 1828. Within a year of his inauguration, Derbigny was killed in a carriage accident.[i]

On March 1, 1813, Hall and Mathews convened the Supreme Court in New Orleans for the first time. They sat just long enough for them to swear their oaths and to hear a public recitation of their commissions. Because Hall's appointment preceded Mathews's appointment by one day, he took up the role of presiding judge. Both of them appreciated the necessity of a prompt transition from the territorial judiciary, and within a matter of days, they set the change in motion. One of their first steps was to provide timely regular order, and to that end they picked "a Committee to draw up Rules & Regulations for the Government of this court."[j] Its members were François-Xavier Martin (1762–1846), Edward Livingston (1764–1836), Abraham R. Ellery (fl. 1808–?), Étienne Mazureau (1777–1849), and Abner L. Duncan (fl. 1813–1820) (Boudreaux, 1-16). Their stature in New Orleans legal circles and beyond suited the five to the task at hand.

Martin had just left the now extinct Superior Court to become the state's first attorney general. Originally from Marseilles and of a mercantile family, Martin left France for fruitless business ventures in Martinique and New York City. Penniless, he wound up in New Bern, North Carolina, where he became a printer, and by the 1790s he was one of the foremost printers in that state. He published a line of popular law books, including statutes, law reports, treatises, and the first English translation, his own, of the revered French civilian commentator Robert Pothier's highly esteemed *Traite des obligations selon les regles tant du for de la conscience que du for extèrieur.* Printing law books prompted Martin to study law.

Admitted to the North Carolina bar as "Frank X. Martin," he quickly became renowned for his formidable advocacy and was respected for his weighty scholarship that drew deeply from the common and civil law. President Madison appointed him to the bench in the Mississippi territory before he transferred him to the Superior Court in New Orleans. Martin joined the Supreme Court in 1815 and stayed for over thirty years, the last ten of which as chief judge.[k]

FRANÇOIS-XAVIER MARTIN *from the Louisiana Supreme Court Portrait Collection, Law Library of Louisiana, New Orleans.*

Livingston was Martin's opposite. To the manor born, he descended from a potent clan of Scots immigrants whose members had dominated New York state politics as far back as the seventeenth century. The revolutionary war years cost the Livingstons dearly and turned the youthful Edward against all things English. An early exposure to Roman law grew into an ardent belief that civil law was superior to common law. Livingston was on a promising trajectory in state and national politics before allegations that he had embezzled funds from the office of United States attorney forced his sudden disappearance from New York City in 1804. He resurfaced in New Orleans, where his dazzling legal skills quickly made him one of the territory's leading attorneys. His marriage to a refugee widow from Saint Domingue and his festering disputes with Governor Claiborne accounted for his frequent political alliances with the city's *ancienne population* and his devotion to codification of the laws in force.[l]

A Frenchman from La Rochelle, Mazureau became conversant in Spanish law and language during the time he lived in Cádiz. He fell afoul of Napoleon Bonaparte and was jailed. Once released from prison, he sailed to New York City and stayed until he settled in New Orleans. By 1805, he was an established attorney who often collaborated with Derbigny and Livingston. Like them, he was a firm advocate for codification and the retention of civil law in Louisiana. One of the authors of the Constitution of 1812, he succeeded Martin as attorney general and represented New Orleans in the General Assembly before his death in 1849.[m]

As for Ellery and Duncan, there are only remnants of either man's existence. Certain it is that Ellery was living in the city by 1808 because he was noted as occupying office space in the Customs House by that date, and that location suggests interests in overseas business, a practice in commercial law, and the occasional hawking of contraband under the table. Duncan arrived in town some time before or just after the Louisiana Purchase. Clients dealt with him at his office on Royal Street. Who they were is a mystery except for Vincente Folch, who was the governor of Spanish West Florida. Duncan arranged to provide Folch with 1,300 barrels of flour, which violated the federal Embargo Act of 1807. None of the local authorities noticed; they engaged in smuggling too. In any case, both men were well regarded enough for Hall and Mathews to put them on the rules committee.[n]

The committee not only drew on the wisdom of its members: it bred a pride of ownership in the Supreme Court and became a model for future uses. It finished its work in about a week's time. Unfortunately, there are no longer any minutes of its deliberations or copies of its report to Hall and Mathews, although a route to the final "Rules & Regulations" may be mapped with a degree of certainty. Martin probably would have acted as chairman.[2] If so, then he would have urged consideration of the Superior Court rules for a pattern. They were handy, they were familiar to Hall, Mathews, and members of the bar, and they could readily be tailored to fit the Supreme Court. Those were not inconsequential considerations, given the haste with which the court began.

Workable rules were needed promptly in order to move its business in a tidy way and to lessen the muddle that invariably accompanied the opening of any new court.[30] Accordingly, regarding Martin as the prime mover seems self-evident. That conclusion is further reinforced by the speed with which the rules were drawn up and promulgated.

Their next move came when Hall and Mathews validated the credentials of fifty-eight lawyers who had been licensed by the defunct Superior Court.[3] That step activated the Supreme Court's administrative supervision of the bar. Still to be determined were the qualifying standards for subsequent applicants but defining them with greater precision than the presently acceptable norms was put off to another day. In 1813, the prevailing credentials demanded for admission to the bar were modest: good character, citizenship, residency, and suc-

---

2 The supposition that Martin chaired the committee is based upon this fact. It was customary for American practice to record committee members in order of precedence. Whoever came first chaired, and the rest were listed in order of their rank.

3 That number derives from an in-house finding aid "Roster of Attorneys, 1813–1930." The "Roster" was compiled in an Excel spreadsheet by the late Marie E. Windell and other library personnel from the minute books in the Historical Archives of the Supreme Court of Louisiana, Earl K. Long Library, University of New Orleans. Reasonably accurate, it is not always consistent. I am indebted to Georgia Chadwick for making a copy for me.

cess at passing an oral bar examination. Evidence of an education from an out-of-state law school was also acceptable as it often provided better schooling than the more common methods of self-study or apprenticeship. Immigrant lawyers in good standing and licensed in their home states were readily admitted, provided they could demonstrate their familiarity with Louisiana law and practice.[p] An important addition to rules came in 1821, when the court banned applications from "gentl[e]men not acquainted with the legal language of the State."[q][4] Pointedly aimed at French speakers who refused to learn English, it forced them to choose between mastering it or not being admitted to practice. That the rule was promulgated suggests the existence of numerous French-speaking lawyers who refused to master English and that refusal prompted the rule. And without saying so directly, the General Assembly codified the rule in 1822.[r]

During the early years, the Supreme Court kept pace because the requests for bar examinations were manageable and the number of appeals was small. But from the 1820s onward it floundered as the judges strained to dispatch accelerating workloads. They fell farther and farther behind as banks, railroads, and steamboats came to the state. As lawyers, legislators, and regulators devised new jobs, new laws, and new institutions, those changes inevitably increased the volume of appeals that went to the court. A growing population, an economy unsettled by the Panics of 1819 and 1837, and a flood of applicants for admission to the bar added greatly to the workload in both supreme court districts.[s] Notwithstanding their adherence to the rigid meeting schedules that governed the two circuits, the judges never served the western district

4 The "legal language" was English. That veiled reference to English derived from a mandate in La. CONST. of 1812, art. VI, § 15 that required all statutes, public records, and judicial proceedings "shall be promulgated, preserved and conducted in the language in which the constitution of the United States is written." Couching the wording in euphemism was a bow to the sensibilities of Franco-Louisianans that did not have its intended effect.

adequately, and that was a perennial source of irritation.

The work environment and the judges' work habits were partly to blame. Unlike today's justices, the antebellum judges had none of the secretaries, law clerks, librarians, and other administrative personnel that support the modern court. Access to private law libraries was minimal, especially outside of New Orleans. Rented space doubled as chambers because the Supreme Court lacked a fixed residence until it moved into the courthouse on Royal Street in 1910.[5] The state appropriated modest funds for books, paper, pens, ink, and not much more, although it did reimburse the judges for travel expenses whenever they went on the circuit. Whether deciding cases, writing opinions, or testing would-be lawyers, the judges worked at a leisurely pace. Their work week was a mere three days long. Lengthy oral arguments, colloquies among themselves and byplay with the attorneys, and rehearings dragged on for hours at a time. So did the bar examinations. Advancing years and declining health were another impediment. Mathews was beset by illnesses that caused frequent absences that left the court unable to muster a quorum, such as when he missed most of 1829. Stubbornly refusing to stand down, he retired only after death called him to a higher bench.[t] An equally aged, nearly sightless Martin missed half of the 1835 terms while he was in Paris seeking corrective surgery. The operation failed, and he was totally blind when he succeeded to the

5 The Court moved quite a lot before settling into the Royal Street building. Between 1813 and 1827, it occupied space in Government House, which sat at Toulouse and Levee Streets and which also housed the governor and the legislature. Then it had a room in the Capitol Building at Baronne and Common Streets. It remained there sometime after the capital was removed to Baton Rouge in 1848, and then it went to the Sala Capitular in the Cabildo. Came the Civil War, it decamped to Opelousas, Alexandria, and Shreveport before it returned to the Cabildo where it stayed until 1910.

chief judgeship.[u][6] Other absences often led to months-long delays, and obstinate as ever, he would not retire.[v]

At his best, Martin always was a difficult colleague who countenanced few improvements to the Supreme Court's routines. His stubbornness drove off George Eustis[7], Mathews's replacement, who lasted for a mere four months before he quit in disgust. Aside from Rice Garland, the old chief judge intimidated the new ones who came to the court after the General Assembly raised its size from three to five members in 1839. In truth, Martin tolerated only Alexander Porter[8] and Henry Adams Bullard. A Massachusetts native, Bullard (1788–1851) attended Harvard College, studied law in Pennsylvania, and became a Philadelphia lawyer. He was recruited by a Spanish revolutionary in 1813 for what turned into an abortive attempt at liberating Mexico that nearly led to his death. Sorely wounded, he escaped to Natchitoches, Louisiana, with little beyond his legal skills. While his health improved, he learned local law and customs and grew a thriving law practice. Politics beckoned as his reputation in Natchitoches and the surrounding region widened. A founder of the Whig Party in Louisiana, he served as a member of the General Assembly,

---

6 The state House of Representatives authorized the absence.

7 George Eustis (1796–1858) was a Bostonian. As a young man he attended Harvard College and studied law in the Hague before he moved to New Orleans. Admitted to the bar in 1822, he established a successful law practice and became active in politics as a Jacksonian Democrat. He was secretary of state and attorney general before his brief tenure on the Martin Court, and he was the first chief justice of Louisiana. See Shull, *Chief Justices of Louisiana*, 13-15.

8 Alexander Porter (1785–1844) was from Donegal, Ireland. He emigrated to Tennessee where he became an attorney. Acting on advice from Andrew Jackson, he removed to the Orleans Territory and, despite not being naturalized, he became an architect of the Constitution of 1812. He joined the Supreme Court in 1821 and stayed until his election to the Senate of the United States in 1833. See Wendell Holmes Stephenson, *Alexander Porter: Whig Planter of Old Louisiana* (Baton Rouge, 1934); Joseph G. Tregle Jr., "Through Friends and Foes with Alexander Porter," *Louisiana History*, 3 (1962):184-85.

and the United States House of Representatives. During his career, he also served as secretary of state and as a district court judge. Teaching attracted him too, and after he left the Supreme Court for good in 1846, he became the founding dean and professor of civil law at the University of Louisiana Law School, ancestor of the Tulane University School of Law.[w]

HENRY ADAMS BULLARD from the Louisiana Supreme Court Portrait Collection, Law Library of Louisiana, New Orleans.

Martin's extraordinary regard for Bullard as one of his few friends stemmed from more than his affection for lawyering and judging; their affinity for scholarship and legal education drew them close. Martin was the first reporter of the Supreme Court's decisions as well as the author of a two-volume history of the state. Bullard collaborated with Thomas Curry to compile a digest of state statutes, and he wrote a short biography of Martin.[x] As educators, they used their rule-making authority to tighten standards in the hope that stricter requirements would slow the flood of applications for bar examinations. The General Assembly's addition of the two additional judges was no more successful in halting the torrent than had been the medieval English King Cnut in staying the North Sea tide, and the inundation threatened to overwhelm the Supreme Court. During the first nine months of 1840, the judges approved fifty-eight new attorneys in New Orleans plus an unknown number in the western district. (There is no tally of the failed examinees.)[y] Confronted with a problem that was only to worsen, even Martin accepted the necessity of tinkering with the rules. In November 1840, the Supreme Court issued a new rule that updated admission requirements. Besides proof of good character, candidates were now required to demonstrate their knowledge of Louisiana law and practice by passing a test on a prescribed "Course of Legal Studies." The examination would be conducted four times a year in New Orleans and once in Opelousas by a screening committee that would consist of seven local attorneys. Certified candidates would then sit for a public examination by the judges, and the successful ones would receive their licenses. Étienne Mazureau, George Eustis, George Strawbridge[9], Pierre Rost-Denis[10], John Randolph Grymes, and Levi Pierce[11] constituted the first New Orleans examining committee, and given who they were, they likely helped with drafting the rule.[z]

---

9 George Strawbridge (1785-1859) was a Marylander who sat on the Court from August to December 1839. He then became a judge of the Fourth District Court in New Orleans.

10 Pierre Adolphus Rost-Denis (1797–1869) was a Frenchman who emigrated to Natchez in 1816. By 1822 he was living in Louisiana when he was a member of the General Assembly. He sat on the Court from March to June 1839 and again from 1846 to 1853. During the Civil War he was the Confederacy's commissioner to Spain.

11 Levi Pierce (1796–1866). Later he was secretary of state during the Roman administration but he never held other public offices. See *The Times-Democrat* (New Orleans, La.), April 6, 1866: 2.

George Eustis from the Louisiana Supreme Court Portrait Collection, Law Library of Louisiana, New Orleans..

An improvement, to be sure, the rule of 1840 did not have the desired effect, as the number of applications continued to rise, which only added to a relentless clamor for renovations that would align the Supreme Court with current realities. Those complaints came from several directions. The literate citizenry took to the press to castigate the judges' perceived slothfulness, which seemed a denial of justice and fairness. Legislators decried their inability to provide remedies because of the Constitution of 1812 that had no mechanism for amendment; Democrats saw an opportunity to seize power from the Whigs by eliminating the constitutionally imposed property requirement for suffrage. Then there was a loosely strung group of lawyers who argued forcefully for the necessity of a thoroughgoing law reform that even included a new constitution. Among the more vocal of these reformers were Gustavus Schmidt, George Eustis, Isaac Edward Morse, E. A. Canon, and Solomon W. Downs. Eustis favored imposing term limits on the judges and assigning specific administrative responsibilities to a chief justice. Morse complained about the Court's deficiencies in the western supreme court district, which, in his estimation, the judges all too frequently neglected.[aa] Canon[bb] and Downs[cc] argued for improvements to the state's criminal law and for the creation of some means to hear criminal appeals. (Their complaints contributed to the short-lived Court of Errors and Appeals that the General Assembly erected in 1843.[dd]) Schmidt was the most astringent critic of all. Indeed, such was his ire that he founded *The Louisiana Law Journal*, which began in 1841. It was the first of its kind in the lower South, and it was not only Schmidt's vehicle of attack: it also gave voice to others of like mind.[12]

Such was the mounting force of the complaints that by the middle of the 1840s, it was no longer politically possible to ignore them. In March 1844, the General Assembly enacted a call for an election of delegates to meet as a constitutional convention that August.[ee] Instead of convening in New Orleans, where they would be tempted to debauch themselves, the delegates assembled about one hundred miles away, in the small town of Jackson in East Feliciana Parish. The meeting was short, but before it adjourned until January 1845, the delegates elected officers and adopted an exhaustive set of procedural rules, one of which called for a committee to recommend changes to the existing judiciary article.[13] John Randolph Grymes chaired that committee, which included George Eustis, Isaac T. Preston, and George Rogers King. The Grymes committee began deliberating shortly after the convention reassembled in New Orleans.

12 Schmidt (1795–1877) contracted with a New Orleans printer called Emile Johns as his publisher only to have Johns liquidate his business. Consequently, there was but a single volume, consisting of four issues, published between May 1841 and April 1842. On Schmidt as a lawyer, scholar, and book collector. See M.H. Hoeflich and Louis de la Vergne, "Gustavus Schmidt: His Life & Library," *Roman Legal Tradition*, 1 (2002): 112-22. See also Warren M. Billings, "Gustavus Schmidt and *The Louisiana Law Journal*," *Unbound: A Review of Legal History and Rare Books*, 12, No.2 (2020-21):6-19.

13 For a detailed treatment of the convention's entire proceedings, the whole content of the constitution, its ratification, and its repeal see Judith Kelleher Schafer, "Reform or Experiment? The Constitution of 1845," in Billings and Hass, *In Search of Fundamental Law*, 21-37.

Unlike their predecessors in the first constitutional convention, Grymes and his colleagues had a clear-eyed view of the role of contemporary supreme courts and their place in state governments, and they debated draft resolutions that corresponded with that vision. Their hearings alternated with similar discussions on other articles until May, when the convention adopted the new constitution in its entirety.[ff]

Although the two Supreme Courts shared similarities, the one that emerged from the Grymes committee hearings and the convention debates was decidedly different. Whereas the old constitution had assigned judicial power merely to "a supreme court and inferior courts," that authority was now vested in "a supreme court, in district courts, and justices of the peace."[gg14] Both documents assigned the Supreme Court "appellate jurisdiction only" in civil matters involving at least three hundred dollars.[hh] (During the convention, there had been a failed attempt to raise the threshold to five hundred dollars as a way to limit appeals.) That power was extended to granting writs of habeas corpus and to hearing criminal cases "on questions of law alone, whenever the punishment of death or hard labor may be inflicted, or when a fine of three hundred dollars may actually be imposed" (La. CONST.: 8).

Integrating the American writ of habeas corpus had proven unsuccessful in 1812, and so had later attempts to embrace it statutorily. When the issue arose in the constitutional convention, the delegates were at first reluctant to grant the power to the Supreme Court. Seemingly, there was nothing in contemporary Louisiana law on which to model

14 *The Constitution of Louisiana* is a pamphlet copy bound in a volume called *The Constitutions of Louisiana, 1845-68* that is in the Widener Library at Harvard University. That and a copy of the other three constitutions came into the possession of the poet Henry Wadsworth Longfellow who taught at Harvard. Either he or his daughter, Alice M. Longfellow, bound them together. It was she who gifted the volume to Harvard as is evident from the bookplate on one of the front free leaves.

the right or if granting it should it be entrusted to the court, but it was incorporated after lengthy debates.

Assigning criminal appeals to the high court answered reformers' complaints and eliminated the need for the Court of Errors and Appeals. Then, too, in the context of 1845, restricting the Supreme Court's criminal jurisdiction to questions of law alone had a clear logic behind it. Clerks of the district courts preserved few accurate records of testimony or physical evidence introduced at trials, meaning that there was no way to certify on appeal what witnesses said or what evidence was presented for or against a defendant. Such as they were, criminal law and practice were backward and outdated. The only guide to practice was Lewis Kerr's commentary on the Territorial Crimes Act of 1805, *An Exposition of the Criminal Laws of the territory of Orleans: The Practice of the Courts of Criminal Jurisdiction, the Duties of Their Officers, With a Collection of Forms for the Use of Magistrates and Others*, which was out of print.[ii] There was no compilation of the criminal statutes before Merritt M. Robinson published his digest in 1841.[jj] Moreover, most attorneys seldom dealt with criminal law, and neither had many of the judges.[15]

The size of the new court was reduced from five to four: a chief justice and three associates. Seen as an economic move, it was adopted in part to justify raising the justices' salaries to 6,000 dollars for the chief and 5,500 dollars for each of the associates. Instead of an elective judiciary, which some in the convention had wanted, the right of appointment remained

15 Every subsequent constitution retained the restriction. Its wording remained virtually unchanged until the convention that wrote the Constitution of 1974 tried to abolish it. During the debates on the judiciary article a proposal to allow the Supreme Court to review questions of facts as well as law came up for debate, but it went down to defeat after a short discussion. See *Documents of the Louisiana Constitutional Convention Relative to the Administration of Criminal Justice*, 431-34, Law Library of Louisiana. Ultimately the wording reads that "in criminal matters [the Supreme Court's] appellate jurisdiction extends to only to questions of law" (La. CONST. of 1974, art. V, §5b).

with the governor but with a significant break with the past.[kk] Rather than sitting for life, the new justices were limited to staggered tenures of eight years. Term limits achieved one of George Eustis's main goals for constitution reform. As in the past, the justices would continue to be impeachable. Their rule-making and supervisory powers were unchanged. The requirement to sit in New Orleans from November to June remained. Now, however, the justices were permitted to adjust their itinerary in the western circuit according to need rather than the old, rigid, four-month schedule, and that provision appears to have appeased a majority of the western convention delegates.

On paper, the judiciary article erected a Supreme Court that vastly improved upon the one it would replace. The changes it instituted brought the court in line with high courts elsewhere in the nation, which had been one of the reformers' principle objectives. Taking criminal appeals and issuing writs of habeas corpus improved the quality of justice. Rotation in office foretold a periodic infusion of new blood. New blood prevented the stagnation and complacency that had so vexed the Martin Court. Designation of a "chief justice" altered the nature of the court's presiding officer. He not only presided but was given supervisory responsibilities for his court and the courts below as well. That change enhanced his position as the top administrator in the judiciary and the head of the third branch of state government.

None of this would translate from paper to reality without the voters' consent. Seeking their will, Governor Alexandre Mouton called a special election for the fall. In the runup to the poll, a scandal involving Judge Rice Garland intensified the electorate's scorn for the Martin Court and helped to ratify the new constitution. Garland (1798–1863), was a Virginian and a lawyer who had emigrated to New Orleans in 1822. Unlucky in the city, he moved to Saint Landry Parish, near the town of Opelousas. When the Supreme Court came to town, the judges licensed him after he presented his credentials from the bars of

Virginia and North Carolina. He hung out his shingle and married a well-fixed local woman, Céleste Genevieve Lestrapes. His practice led to affiliations with Henry Adams Bullard and other prominent locals, including his father-in-law, who were among the organizers of the Whig Party in the state.

When, in 1834, Bullard traded his seat in the United States House of Representative for another on the Supreme Court, Garland was elected to succeed him. Garland sat for three terms, during which he became a national spokesman for the Whigs and one of the party's primary fundraisers, but he also gained unsavory renown for brawling with House colleagues. He abandoned Céleste Genevieve and their children and took up with his landlady, a married woman called Lucinda Crandall Denny. Their liaison was an open secret that attracted little gossip in Washington social circles and even less notice in Louisiana, where it was commonplace for husbands to keep mistresses and separate households. Nevertheless, the affair started him on a path to his undoing.

Straitened finances caused Garland to leave Congress. With the contrivances of Governor André Bienvenue Roman and Henry Adams Bullard, he went to the Supreme Court, which guaranteed a lifetime appointment and an annual salary of five thousand dollars. In the summer of 1840, he headed off for New Orleans with a heavily pregnant Lucinda and their daughter Eliza Alice in tow. (Their second daughter, Virginia Elizabeth, was born en route.) He joined the Supreme Court in Opelousas in September 1840 and immediately threw himself into clearing the dockets. A healthy hungriness for his work made him a tireless judge who produced speedy opinions and rarely missed sittings. Indeed, during his five-year tenure, he wrote around four hundred majority opinions and at least a dozen dissents. His output neither dented the backlog of cases nor reduced the numbers of new appeals, and it did nothing to quiet the clamor that led to the constitutional convention.

As the constitutional convention did its work, Garland realized the precariousness of his situation. A new Supreme Court had no place for him. There was no chance of an appointment as chief justice or one of the associates. Democrats controlled the legislature, and they would hardly be expected to favor a Whig of his standing. He would be off the Supreme Court and lose his salary. That reversal of fortune would impose swift, severe financial hardship on the Garlands, who lived extravagantly and borrowed to the hilt. Caring for the children who came after Virginia Elizabeth and an illegitimate daughter whom he begot by an enslaved woman added to his need for a reliable source of cash. Whether driven by desperation, arrogance, or stupidity, Garland chose forgery as the way out of his tightening bind.

In the fall of 1845, he forged a note for six thousand dollars and drew it on the account of John McDonogh. One of the wealthiest merchants in the city, McDonogh was also a known business associate of Judge Martin. A broker bought the note only to discover that McDonogh rejected it as a forgery. Attempting to hide his misdeed, Garland returned the unspent cash and pleaded with the merchant not to expose him. McDonogh, pleased to have a Supreme Court judge in his pocket, took back the forged note, destroyed it, and gave Garland two thousand dollars to tide him over. Both men agreed to keep silent. Garland went into seclusion, but rumors of a cover-up leaked to the newspapers. The rumor mill ran full bore after McDonogh's inept denial until the judge's stout disavowal of wrongdoing momentarily slowed it. The drumbeat of rumors and press coverage climaxed on December 8. Court was sitting that morning; spectators jammed the courtroom, and when Garland tried to take his seat, Judge Martin abruptly adjourned the session. Garland protested, shouting that he had come to clear his good name. Martin and his colleagues retired. Garland remained, still proclaiming his innocence while promising the astonished onlookers that he would produce documents that would clear him of all suspicion.

The episode alarmed Judge Martin, but he declined to investigate. Instead, he sought the assistance of Attorney General Isaac T. Preston. Preston launched an informal probe that was inconclusive but which convinced him that Garland had done something illegal. He appointed a commission of examining magistrates that was empowered to take sworn depositions from Bullard, McDonogh, Martin, and the broker and to assemble anything else they deemed pertinent. If the evidence warranted they were to summon Garland before the sitting grand jury for Orleans Parish. Bullard and Martin were spared from testifying because when McDonogh and the broker were deposed, they left no doubt that Garland was a forger and a liar who had shamed the Supreme Court and willfully deceived the public. On December 10, the grand jury issued a warrant for Garland's arrest on suspicion of forgery. Fearful of a messy public trial, a conviction, and jail time, Garland jumped off a steamboat, but his attempted suicide was foiled by a deckhand who pulled him from the Mississippi River. He decamped for parts unknown until he alighted in Texas, where he lived in obscurity for the remainder of his days.

No one had done more to advance Garland than had Henry Adams Bullard. Neither was anyone as close. They were mentor and protégé, they were allies, and they were friends. Garland even called a son "Henry," and that son married Bullard's daughter. He never sought Bullard's forgiveness. Bullard kept any feelings of sadness and betrayal to himself. He surrendered his judicial commission and taught law. More successful at professing than at managing his finances, he died a bankrupt.[11]

Garland's scandal drew the public's attention to the Martin Court as never before. The voters barely ratified the new constitution, and the old Court unraveled in the interval between ratification and the launch of the new government. Martin, months shy of his eighty-fourth birthday, died in December. In mid-February 1846, Bullard, Pierre Rost-Denis, and George Rogers King adjourned the Supreme Court *sine die*. They surrendered their commissions to the new Governor Isaac Johnson and retired to private life.

In 1813, the Supreme Court of Louisiana was untested. Written into the Constitution of 1812 to facilitate statehood, it was accepted by the Americans, few of whom quite understood its purposes. It was disdained by the *ancienne population* as the outsider's threat to their legal customs. That threat appeared all the more real because of the court's strange procedures that were conducted in English. The judges and the lawyers seemed a suspicious lot too, for not one of them was a native-born Louisianan, and they were mostly Americans anyway. Well aware of the tensions, Dominick Hall and George Mathews bonded with New Orleans attorneys for devising administrative rules. In time, the bond tightened, especially as the steady immigration of lawyers in the 1820s, 1830s, and 1840s raised pressing issues about legal education and admissions to the bar. Throughout those years, the court continued to look to New Orleans appellate attorneys for advice. Their advice dictated who might join the bar even as it failed to curb applications, and that failure compounded complaints about the court's shortcomings. Nevertheless, the justices of the new Supreme Court did not break the bond. They would rely on it when they rewrote the rules and encouraged the founding of the New Orleans Law Association (NOLA).

NOTES

a. Junius P. Rodriguez, "Claiborne, William Charles Coles (1775-1817)," *American National Biography* (2001): https://doi.org/10.1093/anb/9780198606697.article.0200064https://doi.org/10.1093/anb/9780198606697.article.0200064

b. US Congress, "An Act Erecting Louisiana into Two Territories, and Providing for the Temporary Government Therof." *U.S. Statutes at Large* 6th *through* 12th *Congress*, 2 (1799-1813): 283-290, Library of Congress; $_{WB}$Mark F. Fernandez, *From Chaos to Continuity: The Evolution of Louisiana's Judicial System, 1712–1862*, 1st ed. (Baton Rouge, 2001), 16-47.

c. Warren M. Billings, "From This Seed: The Constitution of 1812" in $_{WB}$*In Search of Fundamental Law: Louisiana's Constitutions, 1812-1974*, ed. Warren M. Billings and Edward F. Haas (Lafayette, 1993).

d. $_{WB}$Cecil B. Morgan, comp. "Constitution of Form of Government of the State of Louisiana" in *The First Constitution of the State of Louisiana*, (New Orleans, 1975).

e. "An Act to Organize the Supreme Court of the State of Louisiana, and to Establish Courts of Inferior Jurisdiction," La. § 17-18 in *Acts of Louisiana, 1813*: 28, HeinOnline.

f. $_{WB}$Warren M. Billings, ed. *Historic Rules of the Supreme Court of Louisiana, 1813-1879* (Lafayette,1985), xvii.

g. $_{WB}$Janice Shull, *The Chief Justices of Louisiana: Life Sketches* (New Orleans, 2007), 1-3.

h. $_{WB}$Shull, *The Chief Justices of Louisiana*, 4-8; $_{WB}$Fernandez, *From Chaos to Continuity*, 46-47.

i. George Dargo, "Derbigny, Pierre Auguste Charles Bourguignon, (1767-1829)," *American National Biography* (2000): https://doi.org/10.1093/anb/9780198606697.article.0300135; Joseph Tregle Jr. "The Governors of Louisiana: Pierre Auguste Charles Bourguinon Derbigny 1828-1829." *Louisiana History: The Journal of the Louisiana Historical Association*, 22, no.3, (1981): 298; Judith Fenner Gentry, "Pierre August Bourgignon Derbigny," *Dictionary of Louisiana Biography Online*: Louisiana Historical Society.

j. $_{WB}$Sybil Ann Boudreaux, "The First Minute Book of the Supreme Court of the State of Louisiana, 1813 to May 1818: An Annotated Edition" (master's thesis, University of New Orleans, 1983), 1-16.

k. Michael G. Chiorazzi, "François-Xavier Martin: Printer, Lawyer, Jurist," *Law Library Journal*, 80 (1988): 63-99; Judith Schafer, "Martin, François-Xavier (1764-1846), jurist and author," *American National Biography Online* (2000): https://doi.org/10.1093/anb/9780198606697.article.1100558; Kathy T. Dugas, "An Immigrant's Journey to Wealth and Power: The Story of François-Xavier Martin," *Louisiana History: The Journal of the Louisiana Historical Association*, 50, no.3 (2009):321-40.

l. $_{WB}$William B. Hatcher, *Edward Livingston: Jeffersonian Centurion in the American Southwest* (Baton Rouge, 1940); Marie Windell, "Edward Livingston," *Dictionary of Louisiana Biography Online*: Louisiana Historical Society; Alexander De Conde, "Edward Livingston (1764–1836) lawyer and politician," *American National Biography Online* (2000): https://doi.org/10.1093/anb/9780198606697.article.0300286

m. Jane B. Chaillot, "Étienne Mazureau," *Dictionary of Louisiana Biography Online*: Louisiana Historical Society.

n. Isaac Joslin Cox, "General Wilkinson and his Later Intrigues with the Spaniards," *The American Historical Review*, 19, no.4 (1914): 807, https://doi.org/10.2307/1836831; David Hart White, *Vicente Folch, Governor in Spanish Florida, 1787-1811* (University Press of America, 1981).

o. *Acts of Louisiana, 1805*: 219-60, HeinOnline; Mark F. Fernandez, "The Rules of the Courts of the Territory of Orleans," *Louisiana History: The Journal of the Louisiana Historical Association*, 38, no.1 (1997): 63-86.

p. Elizabeth Gaspard, "The Rise of the Louisiana Bar: The Early Period, 1813–1839," *Louisiana History: The Journal of the Louisiana Historical Association*, 28, no.2 (1987):183-97.

q. Billings, *Historic Rules of the Supreme Court*, 6.

r. "An Act relative to applicants for a license to practice law," in *Acts of Louisiana, 1822*: 72, HeinOnline.

s. $_{WB}$George D. Green, *Finance and Economic Development in the Old South: Louisiana Banking, 1804-1861* (Redwood City, 1972); $_{WB}$Jeannine E. Douglas, "Steamboats and Slaves: Issues and Liabilities in Louisiana, 1831-1861" (master's thesis, University of New Orleans, 1991); $_{WB}$Bennett H. Wall et al., *Louisiana, A History*, 4th ed. (Wheeling, 2002), 129, 155, 158; $_{WB}$Charles G. Rivet, "Commercial Evolution in the Catahoula Basin with Perspectives on Two Frontier Families" (master's thesis, University of New Orleans, 1997).

t. Louisiana Supreme Court, "Minute Book," Historical Archives of the Supreme Court, 4: 241-43, 477-78.

u. "Joint Resolution of the Senate and House of Representatives," (January 30, 1835) in Acts of La. (1835): 19, HeinOnline.

v. "An Act to increase the number of judges of the Supreme Court of the State of Louisiana," in *Acts of La. (1839)*: 4, HeinOnline.

w. Carl A. Bauer, "Henry Adams Bullard," *Dictionary of Louisiana Biography Online*: Louisiana Historical Association; Dora J. Bauer "The Career of Henry Adams Bullard." *Louisiana Historical Quarterly*, 23, (1940): 999-1106.

x. Carla Downer Pritchett, "Case Law Reporting in Nineteenth-Century Louisiana," in ${}_{WB}$*A Law Unto Itself?: Essay in the New Louisiana Legal History*, ed. Warren M. Billings and Mark F. Fernandez (Baton Rouge, 2001,) 58-59, 60, 62; ${}_{WB}$François-Xavier Martin, *The History of Louisiana* from *the Earliest Period; Volume 2* (New Orleans, 1827-1829); François-Xavier Martin, comp. *Reports of Cases Argued and Determined in the Supreme Court of Louisiana, 1809–1830* (New Orleans, 1846–1851); Henry Adams Bullard and Thomas Curry, eds., *A New Digest of the Statute Laws of the State of Louisiana From the Change of Government to the Year 1841* (New Orleans, 1842); ${}_{WB}$Henry Adams Bullard, *A Discourse on the Life and Character of the Hon. François Martin.*

y. "Roster of Attorneys."

z. Billings, *Historic Rules of the Supreme Court*, 9-11; Warren M. Billings, "A Course of Legal Studies: Books that Shaped Louisiana Law," in, *A Law Unto Itself*, Billings and Fernandez, 1-25. The rule was codified during the legislative session of December 1841, *Acts of Louisiana, 1841*, 516-18, HeinOnline.

aa. Isaac Edward Morse, "Observations on the Present Judiciary System in the Western Districts of the State of Louisiana," *The Louisiana Law Journal*,1, no. 4 (1842):18-22

bb. E. A. Canon, "On the Necessity of a Court of Criminal Appeals," *The Louisiana Law Journal*, 1, no. 2 (1841): 78-83.

cc. Solomon W. Downs, "Notes on Criminal Law," *The Louisiana Law Journal*,1, no.3 (1842): 30-38.

dd. Sheridan E. Young, "Louisiana's Court of Errors and Appeals, 1843–1846," in Billings and Fernandez, *A Law Unto Itself*, 99-117

ee. "An Act to Provide for the Calling of a Convention for the Purpose of Readopting, Amending, or Changing the Constitution of the State" La. in *Acts of La. 1844*, 31-32, HeinOnline.

ff. *Journal of the Convention Called for the Purpose of Re-Adopting, Amending or Changing the Constitution of the State of Louisiana* (New Orleans, 1845), 1-312, HathiTrust. Printed double columns, this version of the *Journal* combines the deliberations of both the Jackson and the New Orleans meetings. The Jackson deliberations begin on page 1. They end at the middle of the left column of page 65.

gg. La. CONST.: 1; La. CONST. of 1845: 8, HeinOnline.

hh. La. CONST.: 8.

ii. Warren M. Billings, "A Neglected Treatise: Lewis Kerr's *Exposition* and the Making of Criminal Law in Louisiana." *Louisiana History: The Journal of the Louisiana Historical Association*, 36, (1997): 452-72.

jj. $_{WB}$Merritt M. Robinson, *A Digest of the Penal Law of the State of Louisiana, Alphabetically Arranged* (New Orleans, 1841).

kk. *Journal of the Convention*, 195-97.

ll. "Scandal in the Court: The Rise and Fall of Judge Rice Garland," *Southern Studies: An Interdisciplinary Journal of the South*, 24, (2017): 1-27.

Chapter Two

The Beginnings Of The New Orleans Law Association

A mere six years, five months, and six days after the voters ratified the Constitution of 1845, another convention rewrote Louisiana's organic law. The judiciary article in the new constitution raised the number of justices from four to five, extended their terms from eight to ten years, and made them subject to popular election. Candidates for chief justice had to run statewide whereas the associates had to stand in one of the state's four new judicial constituencies. There was a proviso that allowed the General Assembly to restrict the justices' jurisdiction in certain areas of civil litigation, but it was never exercised.

On the other hand, however, a mandate in the Constitution of 1852 curtailed the Supreme Court's rule-making authority. It limited oral arguments to four hours, which was clearly meant to put an end to the habitual bent of both justices and lawyers to loquaciousness.[a16] The Constitution of 1852 displaced Chief Justice George Eustis but before he stood down in May 1853, he entrained two changes in the bond between the court and the New Orleans attorneys. He undertook a thoroughgoing overhaul of the court's rules, and the second was his founding of a

16 On the making of the Constitution of 1852, see Wayne M. Everard, "Louisiana's 'Whig" Constitution Revisited: The Constitution of 1852," in WB Warren M. Billings and Edward F. Haas, eds., *In Search of Fundamental Law: Louisiana's Constitutions, 1814–1974* (Lafayette, La., 1993), 37-52.

society that became the New Orleans Law Association (NOLA). Both changes would have lasting consequences for the court, the attorneys, and the shape of the state's legal order.

George Eustis's time on the Martin Court had convinced him of the absolute necessity of recasting the governance of the court, and no sooner than he was chief justice than he charged a committee of New Orleans attorneys to prepare a draft of new rules. Existing records do not reveal the names of committee members, nor do they contain any working papers, or notes of conversations with Eustis, the other justices, and the committee itself, but clues to the unfolding of the new rules are traceable in one of the court minute books and a volume of the *Louisiana Reports*.

The committee went to work in the spring of 1846, and within six months it had come up with a draft that it spread before the justices. Gone was the jumble of repetitive, outdated, unmanageable, and no longer practical rules that were scattered throughout nine minute books. In their place was a three-page compilation of twelve tersely worded, logically arranged rules. Eustis and his colleagues poured over the draft for a month. They embraced most of it, although they made several alterations of their own. Their most significant change was their combination of two draft directives. It amounted not only to a procedural clarification, it shortened the number of rules from twelve to eleven. Then the Court promulgated their revised text on December 7, 1846.[b]

Rules one through three prescribed how briefs were to be filed; they required copies to be given to litigants in a timely manner, and they ordered that each side post appearance bonds. Two rules dealt with how the clerk of court should docket cases and how he should fix the order of their hearing. The next four limited the Court's ability to grant rehearings, and the final two reformed the Court's control of the bar. Rule ten compelled applicants to apply for admission through the clerk who in turn was expected to publish a notice of all applications at least three days before their presentation to the justices for their determination.

The more important rule eleven reorganized the standards of legal education and reset the process of how candidates were to be examined. Applicants would have to meet three personal requirements: proof of U.S. citizenship, written evidence of good character, and, if one were licensed in another state, proof of having lived in Louisiana for a minimum of one year. No matter their origins, every candidate had to demonstrate his mastery of the syllabus of legal studies that the court had devised back in 1840. As in the past, a preliminary examination would be administered by a screening committee of New Orleans attorneys, but with this difference. No longer would the vetting occur at any time when the court was sitting. Henceforth, the justices would appoint a screening committee twice a year. In turn, the screeners would meet two times in every month during court sessions "On the First and Third frydays of each month at 5 Oclock PM."[c] The successful applicants would then be recommended to the justices who would quiz them, and those who withstood that public grilling were "admitted and licensed as an Attorney and Counsellor at Law." Failed candidates could reapply only after they had completed six months of additional training, although there was no limitation on the attempts one might try before giving up.

Eustis's leadership in revising the rules produced the desired effect. Using them relentlessly, he shortened oral arguments, he coaxed his colleagues to pare back the length of their opinions, and he reduced rehearings, all of which made for a more efficient court. So did the modifications of the requirements for bar admissions. Never again was the court swamped by willy-nilly demands for those examinations. Now there was an orderly procedure that ruled one of the court's most important and time-consuming administrative duties. By the time his tenure ended, Eustis had succeeded in restoring public confidence in the court and clearing its backlog of cases. His was an elegant solution that addressed a pressing problem of the moment. What he could not imagine was its long-term effect; it exceeded his original goal and laid beyond his imagination. To be sure there were subsequent modifications, but the Rules of 1846 prevailed until the 1920s before they were supplanted by the precursors of the modern rules of governance.[d]

How Eustis encouraged the society that became the NOLA is difficult to pin down because little in the existing records show his hand. He and the attorneys who drafted the Rules of 1846 probably talked about the usefulness of such a society, and they decided to found one. Such a possibility would not have been out of the question, given Eustis's interest in elevating the reputation of the profession and the attorneys' desire to please him.

Moreover, Eustis and the attorneys were surely mindful of that the passing of their older colleagues had the potential to diminish the bar and that a formal association could sustain their relationship. Equally suggestive, if not more so, was the meeting that occurred at the Supreme Court in the spring of 1847. On an evening that May numerous attorneys responded to an invitation to consider forming just such an association, but no copies exist. The invitation was Eustis's.[17] After Orleans Parish court Judge Charles Watts (1786–1851) gaveled them to order, Alfred Hennen (1786–1870) was chosen temporary chairman, and Thomas Allen Clarke (1814–1894) was selected acting secretary.

Hennen took the chair and called upon another city judge, Edward Rawle (1797–1880). Rawle expressed the desirability of organizing before he introduced a constitution for a society that would promote "the interest, dignity and character" of the city's attorneys and create a law library for the exclusive use of members.[e] After some discussion it was decided that "an association is hereby formed upon the following *Constitution*."

There were twelve parts to that constitution. Articles I

---

17 After Eustis's death, Pierre Rost delivered his *Eulogy Upon the Life and Character of George Eustis Formerly Chief Justice of Louisiana* (New Orleans, 1859) to the NOLA which had it printed for members of the association. The eulogy establishes Eustis's role in founding the NOLA as well as his membership in it.

through IV dealt with the association's purpose and the duties of its officers. The fifth article called for a president to appoint an eight-person Committee on the Library and Disbursements. The committee was to find a suitable room for the library, furnish it, stock it, and employ a librarian. Articles VI, VII, VIII, and IX related to membership. Members would be drawn by invitation from New Orleans. A membership committee would receive nominations and would recommend them for a ballot "by means of black and white balls to be put in a suitable box."

Any candidate who got at least twenty white balls was elected, but one who got three black balls was rejected. Membership fees consisted of a twenty-five-dollar initiation fee and annual dues of five dollars, payable in advance. The membership committee would also receive complaints of "professional delinquency or improper conduct of any member of the bar." Someone who was guilty of such misdeeds was expelled, providing twenty members voted to dismiss him.

Article X fixed meeting dates: The association would meet quarterly, and a quorum was set at thirty members. The eleventh article forbade deficit spending, while the twelfth article specified how the constitution could be amended. An endorsed copy was filed with the recorder of mortgages for Orleans Parish. It proved the existence of the association but nothing else. Who drafted the constitution is anyone's guess. It could have been one of the convenors, a committee of interested attorneys, or possibly George Eustis. The only certainty is that the draft was in hand before the organizing meeting took place.

John Randolph Grymes, Alfred Hennen, and Thomas Allen Clarke were elected president, vice president, and secretary treasurer. Only Rawle, Watts, and five others are identified by name in the constitution—Christian Roselius, Pierre Soulé, Richard Henry Wilde, John Winthrop, and William W. King—and as it is the only record of the founding moment there is no telling who and how many others were present. Eight of the abovenamed ten were prominent legal figures in the city, so their participation lent the association an immediate credibility when it sought members.[18]

Grymes (1786–1854) was of an old-line Virginia family. Like many younger Virginia lawyers, he left the Commonwealth in search of opportunities not found there but that New Orleans offered. Well established before Louisiana became a state, he had close ties to the Supreme Court. Grymes's marriage to Suzette Bosque Claiborne, the widow of former Governor William Charles Cole Claiborne, joined him to the French speaking *ancienne population*. His law practice was largely criminal, and it was one the most lucrative of its day. He was also an inveterate gambler on racehorses, cock fights, and cards.[g]

A Marylander and graduate of Yale College, Hennen (1786–1870) arrived in the city in 1808 and began a law practice. He was one of Andrew Jackson's bodyguards and saw action during the Battle of New Orleans. Like Grymes, Hennen was in the first group of attorneys admitted to practice in 1813, and, again like Grymes, he was close to members of the Supreme Court. Hennen was a leading Presbyterian churchman as well as a banker of some consequence.[h]

Roselius (1803–1870) was a German who left his hometown of Bremen, Germany for New Orleans when he was sixteen. He found work as a printer's apprentice before he began reading law. Admitted to the bar in 1828, he practiced for the rest of his days and developed a keen interest in French civil law and its relationship to the state's law. He was, by turns, a member of the General Assembly, attorney general, and a delegate to the constitutional convention of 1844–1845.[i]

Soulé (1801–1870) fled France to escape imprisonment for his published attack on the Catholic Church. He found refuge in New Orleans in 1826, and having studied law in Toulouse, France, he was easily licensed by the Supreme Court two years

18 The members are identified by name in *Report of the Louisiana Bar Association*, 1:12, 17, HeinOnline.

later. He spent the next two decades developing his practice and financial skills. Politics beckoned and he was elected to the United States Senate where he grew into a sturdy States' Rights Democrat. He left Congress for diplomatic service and in that capacity he was an author of the controversial *Ostend Manifesto.*[19] An outspoken secessionist, he was incarcerated in New York after Union forces captured New Orleans, but he broke parole, fled south, and became an aide-de-camp to General P. G. T. Beauregard. His decision to join the Confederate side ruined him. Wrapped in bitterness and paranoia he died in 1870.[j]

Richard Henry Wilde (1789–1847) was Irish. When he was eight years old, he and his parents left Dublin for Baltimore, Maryland. His father died soon afterwards, at which point his mother took the family to Augusta, Georgia, where Wilde was educated and became a successful lawyer. Law led to politics. A Whig, he was in and out of state government and Congress until 1834, when he lost his bid for reelection to the House of Representatives. Moving to Italy, Wilde dabbled in writing poetry and other literary art forms until his money ran short. He knew people in New Orleans. Believing it might be an advantageous place for a fresh start as a lawyer, he and one of his enslaved people went there in 1844.[k] He encountered Eustis for the first time when Wilde sat for, what he called, a formal test before the Supreme Court that April.[l] Later, in a letter to John Walker Wilde, Richard Henry Wilde described Chief Justice Eustis as "a Democrat, but very much [his] friend."[m] His affiliation with the law association was quite short because he died in September 1847 of yellow fever.

Soulé and Roselius were on the membership committee. They and their unnamed colleagues recruited new members by word of mouth and letters that informed prospects of

---

19 A proposal for the US government to purchase Cuba from Spain that implied the US would war on the Spaniards if they refused to sell. Nothing came of it though it caused a considerable stir in the country.

the nascent association, and its purposes. Undoubtedly, they would have touted the library as a major benefit for members. Another hunting ground was the law department of the University of Louisiana. Eustis had secured a proposal for establishing a university when he was a constitutional convention delegate, and the General Assembly adopted the enabling statute in February 1846. The university board of administrators, which included Roselius, named Henry Adams Bullard dean of the law department. Bullard and three other lawyers—Wilde was one—constituted the faculty. Their curriculum both relied on and expanded the syllabus of 1840 which meant that their graduates had only to show their diplomas to the Supreme Court in order to be licensed. As the library developed students came to depend on it all the more.[n20]

The identity of the early library committee is unknown. So is anything about the library they put together, although funding would not have been an issue because the money from initiation fees and dues were steady sources of income. Despite the absence of records, how the committee went about their task can be sketched out, nonetheless. First of all, they needed space. The committee was given a room near the Supreme Court, which they used until dampness and a leaky roof forced them to relocate elsewhere in the courthouse.[o]

Then, they would have employed workmen—probably enslaved people—to assemble bookcases, reading desks, chairs, and even spittoons. It is very likely those fixtures were recycled furniture from the Supreme Court, or they were bought on the open market.

Next they began the collection. When it grew large enough to merit a librarian they would have hired someone who arranged

20 See *University of Louisiana Law Department* (New Orleans, 1848), which is the earliest known Louisiana law school catalog. It lists the four faculty members, the department rules and regulations, and names of graduates of the class of 1848-1849.

it and assisted patrons. Government documents, statutes, law reports, codes, digests, treatises, foreign language texts, and legal magazines would have comprised the collection, which as it expanded came to include titles not only specific to Louisiana but to other jurisdictions across the nation as well. Items would have been acquired the same way individuals built their private libraries. Some were begged, some were gifted, some were bought new, some were purchased at auction, and some were donations. In fact, two of the earliest acquisitions came from the General Assembly. One acquisition included an order to the secretary of state to deposit and update sets of the statutes, the Supreme Court reports, and certain government documents, in addition to the civil code, and Bullard and Curry's *Digest*. The second was the senate's authorization for the state library to give the association lawbooks that were unnamed.[p] Later library committees expanded the collection throughout the 1850s into one of the larger private libraries in the city.[q]

As the library changed so did the NOLA. By 1855 at least fifty-one lawyers belonged to the association, and there were shifts in the leadership.[r] Ill health forced Grymes out of the presidency just before he died, if not sooner. Joseph Adolphus Rozier[s] succeeded him and Christian Roselius replaced Rozier; other officeholders came and went too. Then there was the decision in December 1855 to change the association from a society of individuals into a state-chartered company under the provisions of "An Act for the organization of Corporations for Literary, Scientific, Religious and Charitable purposes."

The law had gone on the books back in March 1855 largely through the efforts of members of both the NOLA and the directors of the University of Louisiana as a way of helping it and the law department. The act granted six or more individuals the freedom to incorporate as an eleemosynary organization so long as its charter/constitution was registered with an appropriate parochial recorder of mortgages and was vetted by the local district attorney. Like any Louisiana corporation it was self-selecting and self-perpetuating; it enjoyed the right to adopt its own rules and regulations, just so long as nothing in them conflicted with either state or federal constitutions or statutes; and it could sue and be sued. The organization might hold "all manner" of property but the value of those holdings was capped at three hundred thousand dollars.[t]

The existing officers and members incorporated the NOLA "for the purposes of establishing a law library, and of promoting the interest, integrity and honor of the Bar of New Orleans."[u] They agreed to a new charter that was essentially a revision of the original constitution. It was just about as long and had the same arrangement. The association would exist for one hundred years, and it would be domiciled in the Crescent City. Current members retained their places; future membership would be opened exclusively to lawyers who lived or kept offices in Orleans Parish.

Two revisions altered the method of choosing them and disciplining miscreants. Instead of using the old white and black ball system nominees were elected by secret ballot. Ten votes carried an election, but three "no" votes killed a nomination. A lawyer brought up on charges of misconduct was entitled to a hearing before the association, and he was expelled if ten members found against him.

Initiation fees and dues remained the same. Someone who was in arrears for one year and one day forfeited his membership. The officers, the committees, and their responsibilities remained the same. However, one stipulation imposed a new duty on the president of the association and the chairmen of the library and membership committees. Whenever the need arose, the three of them together were to pick someone to represent the association in its affairs or in court, and the chosen person was expected to give "his professional services gratuitously." The last article changed the amending process to guarantee timely notice, advanced copies of proposed amendments, and the approval of at least twenty members who were in good standing. Finally, an addendum transferred all the rights and properties of the existing association to the new one. After Orleans District Attorney B. S. Tappan determined that the constitution met all legal requirements and a copy was filed in the recorder of mortgage's office, it was official.

What happened to the association during the rest of the 1850s is largely conjectural. For certain, it stayed close to the Supreme Court. Members advised the justices on rule changes; they acted as screeners of bar applicants, and some did both.[v] The duties of the president and vice president remained light, so Christian Roselius and Alfred Hennen may have continued in place to the end of the decade. The secretary-treasurer was perhaps the busiest of the five officers. Chairing the library and membership committees was demanding too, but whether Meyer M. Cohen, Edward Rawle, or Joseph Adolphus Rozier left office in 1856 is not known. Apparently, the main effort continued to be increasing the size of the library. The secretary of state continued his updates, other acquisitions came from the usual sources, and the collection was further augmented by a second donation from the state library. By the end of the decade the library was likely among the largest in the city, and it had remained a resource for students in the law department of the University of Louisiana.[w]

The yellow fever epidemic of 1853 thinned the association's ranks. Absent a dues-payer roster one cannot say who died or who were recruited as new members, but the list of incorporators is suggestive, nonetheless. They were a cross section of city attorneys. A few had been at the bar since 1813. Two were retired justices. Another had a seat on the Supreme Court, while several were incumbent district judges. One was a former attorney general. Two were brothers. Several had been or were in the General Assembly. Perhaps, the greater number had emigrated from other states and abroad, or they were native-born Louisianians. As youngsters they would have apprenticed with members who brought them into the association. There were Democrats, Whigs, former Whigs, and a sprinkling of unaffiliated partisans among them.

The association continued to attract little attention from the public or the press. Its comings and goings did not much matter to ordinary citizens who generally regarded attorneys and the law with suspicion and avoided both as much as possible. Newspaper editors knew that articles about scandals and fraught times always drew readers in, and stories about a small legal organization would not. But the lack of notice also resulted from a deliberate calculation on the part of the association itself. From the beginning, keeping a low profile was a matter of policy. Members believed they were most effective when they advocated individually with the Supreme Court or the General Assembly, and that advocacy contributed to a reformation of the criminal statutes.

In the 1840s and 1850s, the Territorial Crimes Act of 1805 was the foundation of the criminal statutes as they existed in Louisiana. The act defined some thirty-two types of offenses. There were guarantees of due process and trial by jury. Protections that were as yet unavailable elsewhere in the nation also promised an affirmative right to an attorney as well as "free access" to counsel at "all seasonable hours." An accused person was also entitled to a copy of the indictment and the jury list at least two days before trial, and he or she could also subpoena witnesses or provide proof of innocence. Furthermore, the law contained an explanation in regards to congressional stipulation on all criminal misconduct "be taken, intended and construed according to the common law of England; and that the forms of indictment, (divested however of unnecessary prolixity) the method of trial; the rules of evidence, and all other proceedings whatsoever in the prosecution of the said crimes, and misdemeanors, changing what ought to be changed, shall be as is by this act otherwise provided for, according to the said common law."[x]

Recognizing the inherent difficulties in such language, In

1805 Governor Claiborne had turned to one of his staff, the Irish American lawyer Lewis Kerr, to publish a commentary on the statute. It was printed in 1806 and was entitled *An Exposition of the Criminal Laws of the Territory of Orleans: The Practice of the Courts of Criminal Jurisdiction, the Duties of Their Officers, With a Collection of Forms for the Use of Magistrates and Others.* Kerr's commentary on the statute did not address the question of the explicit reference to English law, although Kerr remarked at one point that "the common law as recognized in the United States, is no more the law of England than the civil law can now be deemed the law of Rome."[y] Thereby Kerr had seemed to argue that the territorial statute assimilated American law such that it overruled English law whenever the two were at odds. Whatever Kerr's intention, the *Exposition* was the only treatise about the law of crimes until Albert Voorhies published *A Treatise on the Criminal Jurisprudence of Louisiana* in 1860 (Billings, 452-72). Unlike Kerr's book, Voorhies's commentary was a practical how-to book which circumscribed its usefulness as a guide to criminal law or practice.

After 1805, the General Assembly piled statutes upon statutes with little regard to the consequence of its willy-nilly approach to criminal practice. So numerous were the additions that the bench, the bar, and the citizenry were confused about just what was or was not legal. There was no uniform enforcement because in 1813 the Supreme Court was of "the unanimous opinion . . . that [it could] not exercise any criminal appellate jurisdiction," and, despite later challenges, that remained the rule into mid-century.[z] Edward Livingston was engaged to remedy the situation by preparing a criminal code. He worked on his code for more than a decade before he died and the General Assembly postponed codification indefinitely in January 1837.[aa] Subsequently, expanding popular conceptions of the rights of the accused played into the argument. Critics pointed out that the absence of a criminal code effectively nullified the protections promised in the Territorial Crimes Act of 1805. They were meaningless because they were not uniformly enforced by the trial courts so the guilty might go free while the innocent lost liberty or worse. Moreover, criminal practice was sorely hampered by the difficulties in locating texts of the statutes. That perennial roadblock which was eased somewhat after Merritt M. Robinson published his *A Digest of Penal Laws in the State of Louisiana* in 1841. Despite his plea for reform, codifying criminal law was overshadowed by constitutional revision and the other political imperatives throughout the 1840s and 1850s.[bb] Urged on by Robinson, the bench, the bar, Attorney General Isaac E. Morse,[cc] and the press, the General Assembly finally enacted two comprehensive criminal statutes in 1855 that swept away all existing law. The longer of the two, "An Act Relative to Crimes and Offenses," contained 127 definitions of wrongdoing and prescribed the requisite punishment for each offense, which were defined as crimes against persons, property, the state, or public order.[cc] "An Act to Regulate the Mode of Procedure in Criminal Prosecutions" regulated due process and established a first ever basic procedural scheme for trying cases.[dd] Both laws did not meet expectations, but they stood virtually unchanged. Enthusiasm for law reform was giving way to concerns about Louisiana's future in the Union.

As the 1850s closed, members of the NOLA were increasingly caught up in the debates over enslavement and its place in the American republic. As White Louisianans, they knew that their enslaved population and plantation agriculture set their state apart from the North and the West. And because of this, White Louisianans accepted the peculiar institution of enslavement as good and fundamental to their way of living. To the NOLA members, the idea Black people were inferior to White people was an eternal verity, so they were hard put ever to imagine them as equals in any form or fashion. As southern Americans the NOLA members held steadfastly to a constitutional dogma of national union, states' rights, and strict construction that inhibited federal interference with the private property of enslavers.

Challenges to that dogma—Texas' annexation; war with Mexico, who by right could settle the territory captured from the Mexicans; the breakup of the Whig Party; Dred Scott; the rise of the Republican Party; the abominable abolitionists; John Brown's raid on Harper's Ferry—threatened to tear the nation asunder. Talk of secession as the only means of protecting "Southern rights and the Southern way of life" and staving off "northern aggression" grew louder. Events ran rapidly following Abraham Lincoln's election and the South Carolinians attempted to withdraw from the Union. Secessionists pulled Louisiana out of the Union. They prepared for a fight that they easily expected to win. So did the members of the NOLA who flocked to the Confederate standard; the pro-Unionists were passive. War came when General P. G. T. Beauregard's forces fired on Fort Sumter. The association stopped meeting, and now the question was: Would it survive, and if so in what fashion?

NOTES

a. La. CONST. of 1852 art. LXI-LXX: HeinOnline.

b. Louisiana Supreme Court, "Minute Book," Historical Archives of the Supreme Court, 9, (1846-1848): 115-18, 128-31; $_{\text{WB}}$Merritt M. Robinson, comp., *Louisiana Reports* (New Orleans, 1847), 1:ix-xi. The rules are reproduced in $_{\text{WB}}$Warren M. Billings, ed., *Historic Rules of the Supreme Court of Louisiana, 1813–1879* (Lafayette, 1985), 16-21.

c. Billings, *Historic Rules*, 19.

d. Billings, *Historic Rules*, 30-31; La. Ann. 31 (1879): viii; La. Ann. 51 (1899): xxxvi; La. 134, (1914): xii-xiv. A rule change in 1923 finally eliminated the syllabus, which had also been updated from time to time. See La. 152, (1923): vii-viii.

e. La. CONST. of the New Orleans Law Association, (1847) in *Report of the Louisiana State Bar Association*, 1 (1898): 3, 6, HeinOnline

f. La. CONST. of the New Orleans Law Association, 3-6.

g. Ned Hémard, "A New York Hill," in *New Orleans Nostalgia: Remembering New Orleans History, Culture and Traditions* (New Orleans , 2013); Sidney J. Leovy, "The Ante-Bellum Bench and Bar," in *Report of the Louisiana Bar Association, 1899-1900* (New Orleans, 1900), 17-19: HeinOnline.

h. Mary Ann Wegmann, "Jackson's Bodyguards, Lawyers Who Fought in the Battle of New Orleans," Law Library of Louisiana Online: accessed February 21, 2021; Find a Grave: "Alfred Hennen."

i. William H. Adams, "Christian Roselius," *Dictionary of Louisiana Biography Online*: Louisiana Historical Association; Leovy, "The Ante-Bellum Bench and Bar," 18-20.

j. Jay Higginbotham, "Pierre Soulé," *Dictionary of Louisiana Biography Online*: Louisiana Historical Association.

k. John Hollander, *American Poetry: The Nineteenth Century* (New York, 1939), 1:84-86; "Wilde, Richard Henry," *Biographical Directory of the United States Congress, 1774–Online.*

l. Richard Henry Wilde to John Walker Wilde (February 4, 1844) in Edward L. Tucker, ed., "Henry Wilde in New Orleans: Selected Letters, 1844–1847," *Louisiana History: The Journal of the Louisiana Historical Association*, 7 (1966): 340.

m. Wilde to John Walker Wilde (June 16, 1847) in *Louisiana History*, 353.

n. Acts of La., (1846);168; John H. Craft, "The Law Department of the University of Louisiana and Tulane University: Predecessor of the School of Law of Tulane University," unpublished paper, 1978, Tulane School of Law Archives, New Orleans, LA: 1-16.

o. *The Times-Picayune* (New Orleans, LA), June 16, 1854: 5; *The Times-Picayune* (New Orleans, LA), October 6, 1848: 3.

p. Acts of La. (1848): 4; *The Times-Picayune* (New Orleans, LA), December 8, 1848: 2.

q. *The Times-Picayune* (New Orleans, La.), December 8, 1848: 15-17.

r. *The Times-Picayune* (New Orleans, La.), December 8, 1848: 13.

s. Joy J. Jackson, "Joseph Adolphus Rozier," *Dictionary of Louisiana Biography Online*: Louisiana Historical Association.

t. Acts of La. (1855): 185-186, HeinOnline.

u. La. CONST. of 1855 in *Report of the Louisiana Bar Association*, 1:7-13, HeinOnline.

v. Billings, *Historic Rules of the Supreme Court*, 22-23.

w. *The Times-Picayune* (New Orleans, La.), December 8, 1858: 6.

x. "Territorial Acts of Louisiana, 1805," La.: 105, 414-64, HeinOnline.

y. Warren M. Billings, "A Neglected Treatise: Lewis Kerr's *Exposition* and the Making of Criminal Law in Louisiana." *Louisiana History*, 36 (1997): 452-72.

z. Laverty v. Duplessis, 3 Mart. (O.S.) 52, La. 1813; Ogden v. Blackman, La. 1813, 304 (La. 1814); Hyde, et al. v. Jenkins, La. Rep 192 (La. 1834); State v. Judge of the Commercial Court, 15 La. Rep. (La. 1840).

aa. Acts of La. (1821): 30-32, HeinOnline. "Concurrent Resolution of the General Assembly of Louisiana," in *The Complete Works of Edward Livingston on Criminal Jurisprudence . . .*, Edward Livingston, (New York, 1873), 4.

bb. $_{WB}$Merritt M. Robinson, comp., *A Digest of the Penal Law of the State of Louisiana, Alphabetically Arranged* (New Orleans, 1841), iii.

cc. Isaac E. Morse, "Report of the Attorney General, 1854," HathiTrust (1841).

dd. Acts of La., (1855): 130-71, HeinOnline.

ee. Acts of La., (1855): 171-76.

Chapter Three

From the Civil War to Reconstruction to Reorganization

The Civil War made a wasteland of Louisiana. The tally of troops, both Black and White, who died in battle, perishing from wounds and disease, or who survived broken in body and spirit, was incalculable. Across the state the demand for food and shelter took the lives of numberless civilians who succumbed to no place to stay and nothing to eat. The fighting and pillaging tore up roads and bridges, rail lines and rolling stock, levees and port facilities, all of which were vital to recovery but required huge sums of capital to repair. A once flourishing agricultural economy lay wasted. Banks and commercial institutions were ruined. Money and credit were hard to come by, but the greatest of economic blows was the end of enslavement.

The ending of enslavement led to unrelenting efforts by White Louisianans to suppress formerly enslaved people. The goal of suppression was to return Louisiana to White home rule controlled by the Democratic Party. The war reduced the membership of the New Orleans Law Association (NOLA) to a shadow. Union occupation of New Orleans shut the association down for nearly a decade. The association slowly recovered, drew close to the Supreme Court once more, and became the Louisiana Bar Association (LBA). Firmly committed to Jim Crow segregation of the races, members were steeped in pernicious mythology of the Lost Cause that reinforced their unyielding belief in White supremacy.

In 1861, as they prepared for combat, rebel Louisianans gave scant consideration for the consequences of war. To them, fighting would be brief. Valiant, tough Louisiana boys would flock to the colors as one, and they would handily rout the soft Yankees who dared to confront them on any battlefield. Some believed cotton, sugar, and commerce with New Orleans were of such importance to Europeans that the English or the French governments would quickly broker peace between the Union, Louisiana, and the other southern states. Such attitudes ignored how much there was to lose and how little there was to gain. Constitutionally, the federal government was inhibited from interfering with enslavement so long as Louisianans remained loyal, whereas secession ended high protective tariffs for sugar and dealt a heavy blow to the state's economy. The state lacked the infrastructure to produce gunpowder, shotguns, artillery, rifles, side arms, and other supplies on an industrial scale, or anything similar, that could sustain its troops in the field. There was no anticipation of the difficulties in finding replacements for soldiers who were killed, wounded, or deserted, which was evident early in the first year of the conflict.

And no one imagined how easily New Orleans might fall to Union forces. The politicians and the generals reassured themselves that the city could be adequately defended from a riverine invasion. An attacking force would face difficulty in navigating upstream against the always treacherous, fast-moving downriver currents, and without knowledgeable pilots it would find itself aground. Were that obstacle to be overcome the attackers would confront the main line of defense, forts St. Philip and Jackson. The two massive brick strongholds sat on marshy terrain opposite one another along the Mississippi River some seventy miles below town, and their gunners could lay down a gauntlet of withering cannon fire that would drive off enemy invaders. Above the forts were Confederate naval craft that provided an additional barrier. The turn of events in 1862 quickly proved the folly of those strategic assumptions.

Early in 1862 President Abraham Lincoln, Secretary of War Edwin M. Stanton, and Secretary of the Navy Gideon Welles planned to seize New Orleans with a combined force of sailors and infantrymen. Welles appointed Flag Officer David Glasgow Farragut commander of a naval squadron.[a] Stanton gave command of an accompanying army to Major General Benjamin F. Butler (1818-1893). They set out from their base on Ship Island, off the coast of Biloxi, Mississippi, and on April 15, 1862, the battle for New Orleans began. Farragut's mortar schooners opened fire on Fort Jackson. The bombardment went on for a week, but the mortars were ineffective. Against all advice, a frustrated but determined Farragut ran the gauntlet with minimal losses and proceeded to capture, ground, or sink enemy naval vessels that were in his way. On April 25, he dropped anchor just below the city and trained his cannon on the metropolis. His sudden appearance hastened the already chaotic evacuation of military forces, supplies, and people. Secessionist members of the New Orleans Law Association with somewhere else to go left town. The Supreme Court closed up, and the justices took off for the safety of Opelousas. Save for a Unionist judge, Rufus K. Howell, all of the district courts shut down too. Only Mayor John Monroe maintained a vestige of civil authority, and he held off surrendering until April 27, 1862. . Meanwhile General Butler reduced the forts, and on May first he relieved Farragut.[b]

Taking New Orleans was a shiny moment in an otherwise dark spring for President Lincoln. What to do about Union reverses in Virginia and how to protect Washington were more pressing than deciding how to restore New Orleans to its old loyalties. Indeed, neither the president nor his cabinet had given much thought about what to do with the city should the campaign against it succeed. There was general agreement that were New Orleans to be taken then it should remain under martial law until a policy for the restoration of civilian government emerged. It was also agreed that General Butler was the right man to oversee the occupation.

His superiors regarded Butler more for his political skills than for his abilities as a soldier. Of Scotch Irish working-class origins, Butler was born in Deerfield, New Hampshire, but he grew up in Lowell, Massachusetts, where his widowed mother kept a boarding house for female factory workers. After he attended Colby College, Butler read for the bar. Licensed in 1840, he developed into a canny advocate who often relied on stunning ruses to win his cases. He showed no hesitancy in challenging anyone, especially when he was representing the rights of workers. His practice and his activities as a real estate developer made him wealthy. Not unexpectedly, as his reputation spread, he turned his hand to politics.

A staunch Democrat, Butler sat in the Massachusetts General Court (the legislature) and the constitutional convention of 1853. He also attained a general's commission in the Commonwealth's militia. Came the war and he put aside his deep animosities towards Republicans and rallied unhesitatingly to the Union cause. He marched his troops into Maryland, opened a way for Lincoln's safe passage into Washington, and pacified a rebellious Baltimore. Lincoln promoted him to major general and assigned him to Fortress Monroe in Virginia. When some runaway enslaved people came to the fortress he turned aside rebel claims on them. Saying the enslaved people were enemy property, Butler reckoned them "contraband of war" and subject to his seizure. Secretary Stanton sustained him, and his solution was written into federal law as national policy. He was detached to a command that assisted in capturing Hatteras Inlet in North Carolina, and from there he was sent to Ship Island.[c]

Butler faced a troublesome task. He had first to pacify a rebellious citizenry ferociously hostile to the Union cause and the prospect of military rule. Then he had to create a loyal city government and reconstruct an equally loyal judiciary. His initial intention was to subject New Orleans to a fairly moderate regime. In his first proclamation he announced that the city was under martial law, but he expressed a willingness to restore the municipal authorities to their places as soon as feasible and said he would intervene only when military interests were endangered. The courts would continue as before. However, "All disorders and disturbances of the peace done by combinations and numbers and crimes of an aggravated nature, interfering with the forces of the United States" would be tried in a military court.[d]

Mildness failed. From day one, New Orleanians resisted being governed by damn Yankees. Butler cracked down hard and broke the resistance. Butler prosecuted William B. Mumford before a military commission. Accused of high crimes and misdemeanors and treason for desecrating an American flag, Mumford was convicted and condemned to hang. Butler upheld the sentence, and Mumford swung from the gallows. More useful dead than alive to White southerners, the ne'er-do-well Mumford was an early draftee into a pantheon of so-called "martyrs" whose deaths fed the Lost Cause mythology. Butler also imprisoned overtly fractious Confederate sympathizers. His highly controversial General Order No. 28 declared women who harassed his troops as prostitutes and promised to punish them for plying their trade. He seized rebel specie from city bankers and contested the foreign consuls who hid silver, which he eventually confiscated. These and other acts drew world-wide press coverage that reflected unfavorably on Lincoln's government. Repeated rumors that Butler and his subordinates were oppressively corrupt chancers merely compounded the clamor for Butler's scalp, and it was diplomatic pressure that would force Lincoln to replace Butler with Major General Nathaniel P. Banks in December 1862.

Restoring the courts was no less of a challenge. That problem fell mainly to Butler's second in command George F. Shepley. Without informing Butler, Lincoln named Shepley military governor of the city and the parts of Louisiana that Union forces controlled.[21] Lincoln also told no one in Louisiana beforehand

21 A Mainer, George Foster Shepley (1819–1878) was a lawyer turned politician turned army man. He was allied with Butler, though Lincoln kept him on as military governor after he fired Butler. Shepley clashed with General Banks at times, but

of his executive order establishing a provisional district court and naming Charles A. Peabody[22] as its judge. Banks, Shepley, and Peabody were frequently at odds over who had jurisdiction over what, and they clashed repeatedly before Lincoln intervened and quietened the disputes by using his executive power to reopen the federal district court.[e]

In the spring of 1864, Lincoln tested his lenient Ten Percent Plan for restoring the rebel states to the Union as rapidly as possible. Using Louisiana as his model, he ordered General Banks to call for a constitutional convention and an election for a civilian governor and legislature as soon as Banks identified 10 percent of the voters in 1860 who swore their allegiance to the Union. The convention met from April to July. It failed to heed Lincoln's prompting to enfranchise the population of wealthy Black people. However, it did permit the legislature to extend suffrage under certain conditions, but it granted few concessions to Black people of any sorts. The Constitution of 1864 pleased none of the Radical Republicans in Congress, and it was objected by Black Louisianans. Lincoln criticized it too, but his assassination took him off. His successor Andrew Johnson embraced the Constitution of 1864 as he went about pardoning rebels who soon dominated the state legislature and laid even greater restrictions on the Black population. Pressed hard by Black and White Republicans, a reluctant governor recalled the Constitutional Convention in July 1866 to a meeting at Mechanics' Hall. Delegates and their supporters outside

---

Banks could not replace him, and he remained in place until the re-establishment of civilian government under the Constitution of 1864. He resigned from the army in 1866 and later became a United States circuit judge. See Candace Kanes, "George F. Shepley: Lawyer, Soldier, Administrator," *Maine Memory Network Online.*

22 Charles Augustus Peabody (1814–1901) was a New York City and state judge who was an ally of Lincoln's secretary of state New Yorker William H. Seward. See Lyman Horace Weeks, "George A. Peabody," *Prominent Families of New York, Being an Account in Biographical Form of Individuals and Families Distinguished as Representatives the Social, Professional and Civic Life of the City of New York* (New York, 1897), 445, HathiTrust.

the hall were attacked by a mob of White police. Two hours of rioting claimed the lives of 37 Republicans and another 136 were wounded, all but 22 of whom were Black.[f]

Reports of the massacre of peaceful conventioneers and their backers angered congressional Republicans. They wrested control of reconstructing Louisiana and the other southern states from Andrew Johnson and passed the Reconstruction Act of 1867. The act divided the South into five military districts, and General Philip H. Sheridan was given command of the one that included Louisiana. He was empowered to register all adult people–both Black and White–who could swear they had never voluntarily aided the Confederacy. That requirement effectively disenfranchised most White people as it finally extended the vote to Black men. The statute opened the door to what the historian Charles Vincent has observed was the most revolutionary aspect of Reconstruction in the state, Black participation in the writing of the Constitution of 1868.

C. C. Antoine from the Northwest Archives at LSUS.

Black men coalesced with like-minded White delegates to the constitutional convention that drafted a document that departed from earlier statements of Louisiana's fundamental law. It included a bill of rights, a first, that promised the equal enjoyment of those rights to everyone, and it abolished the Black Codes of 1865. Suffrage restrictions excluded most White voters. Women were accorded property rights of their own, and the indigent were supposed to be cared for at public expense. Public whippings; property qualifications for voting and jury duty; and imprisonment for debt were abolished. The number of capital crimes was reduced. Free, integrated public schools, and what became Southern University, were called for. Equal accommodations in business establishments and public transportation were extended to all and sundry without regard to race. There were even provisions for reforming the state militia and giving pensions to surviving veterans of the War of 1812. In the end, however, there was no breakup of plantations or wholesale redistribution of land, although anyone could purchase property if he had money. Titles relating to the executive, legislative, and judicial branches were much the same as those in the Constitution of 1852, which meant that the state government would remain much as it had been before the war.[g]

On paper the Constitution of 1868 may well have been the best statement of Louisiana's fundamental law ever written. However, that is not how it was seen by the majority of White Louisianans after it was put to a vote and approved. White Democrats, including those who belonged to the New Orleans Law Association, relentlessly attacked the Constitution of 1868 as the plaything of undereducated Black people who were being manipulated by corrupt Republicans for their own personal gain. Unhappily, the constitution's dream of a better, equitable society drowned in a gutter of racism, venality, and sleaziness that characterized the politics of postwar Louisiana.

For years after the capture of the city, Joseph A. Rozier

was the titular head of the New Orleans Law Association. His Unionist sympathies probably spared the association's library from being ransacked but there were no meetings until after the war. After E. A. Bradford became president in 1866, he recruited about 150 members and replenished a bankrupt treasury. Under his leadership the members held their collective noses and resurrected the association's ties to the Reconstruction Supreme Court. Some of them contributed to the 1869 revision of the rules and staffed the bar examining committees.[h]

None of that stopped them from openly castigating the Supreme Court for its "specious and unsound" judgments on "racial and public questions."[i] Such other activities as the association engaged in seem to have been expanding the collection, opening the library to students in the University of Louisiana Law Department, and holding annual dinners. On the other hand, there were those who saw different possibilities and wanted to make the association into something else. They took as their model several state organizations that publicly advocated issues of grave professional and political concern to their members before their legislatures. Felix Pierre Poché, Carleton Hunt, and Thomas Jenkins Semmes were among them, and they entrained the slow movement of the New Orleans Law Association into the Louisiana Bar Association.

A native of St. James Parish, Poché (1836–1895) was by turns an attorney, rebel soldier, state senator, and supreme court justice. He graduated from St. Joseph's College, Bardstown, Kentucky, and read law with former Kentucky Governor Robert A. Wickliffe. Admitted to the bar in 1859, he hung up his shingle in St. James Parish but left to fight in the Confederate army. He returned to his practice after the war. Elected a state senator in 1866, he was turned out after the adoption of the Constitution of 1868. Between 1880 and 1890 he sat on the Louisiana Supreme Court. At the time he won a seat in the 1879 constitutional convention, he was already active in trying to revamp the New Orleans Law Association.[j]

FELIX PIERRE POCHÉ from the Louisiana Supreme Court Portrait Collection, Law Library of Louisiana, New Orleans.

Carleton Hunt (1836–1921) was a New Orleanian. His father Dr. Thomas Hunt was a founder of the University of Louisiana medical department. Educated at a local grammar school, Hunt proceeded to Harvard University and the University of Louisiana Law Department before he gained his law license in 1858. A rebel lieutenant in the Louisiana artillery, he was captured and exchanged on condition that he resign. He spent the remainder of the war in New York, Philadelphia, and Baltimore. Afterward, he was a professor and administrator in the University of Louisiana Law Department. He represented Louisiana in Congress (1883–1885) before he returned to New Orleans where he resumed his practice, continued to teach, and was involved in a variety of civic and political activities until his death.[k]

A Washingtonian by birth, Semmes (1824–1899) graduated Georgetown College, read law in a Georgetown law office, attended Harvard Law School, and alighted in New Orleans.

He was an incorporator of the New Orleans Law Association in 1855. A Democrat, he became United States attorney (1858) and the Louisiana attorney general (1859). Elected to the secession convention in 1861, he forcefully advocated leaving the Union and voted for the ordinance to secede. Then he was elected to the Confederate senate where he served throughout the war. Pardoned by President Andrew Johnson, he returned to his law practice and won seats in the constitutional conventions of 1879 and 1898. An interest in legal education led him to accept teaching positions at the University of Louisiana and Tulane University law schools. Stricken by a heart attack he died just as the New Orleans Law Association was reorganizing.[1]

What inspired Hunt, Poché, and Semmes in their attempt to transform the association was their part in founding the American Bar Association (ABA). In 1877, the three of them attended the annual conference of the America Social Science Association in Saratoga Springs, New York, where they joined former Confederate lawyers and attorneys from the northeast who, like them, were socially and politically quite conservative. The conferees were among growing numbers of elite members of the profession nationally who, in the words of a commentator in the *American Law Review*, were determined to stanch a "great democratic flood which [had] been filling the bench with political partisans, the minor legal offices with political hacks, and the bar with an indiscriminate herd of camp-followers."[n] Some had also been acquainted before the war, and they were now anxious to greet one another fraternally, in what they deemed was an honorable profession that transcended their past differences.

Among the attendees was a well-known, well-respected Connecticut jurist and legal educator called Simeon E. Baldwin, who was acquainted with the Louisianans.[n] One evening a casual conversation between Poché and Baldwin led to a suggestion that "It would be a good thing for the legal profession, if there were a special organization, to deal with the subject of jurisprudence in a broader way, in the shape of a national bar association."[o23] Both readily agreed, and they were instrumental in naming a committee that would invite a select group of attorneys, judges, and legal educators to Saratoga Springs in 1878 for the purpose of founding just such an organization. Baldwin acted as committee secretary and drafted a circular letter that was sent around the country. The letter drew the one hundred founders of ABA, which was to be a self-selecting, voluntary organization. In a matter of days a constitution, bylaws, governing structures were agreed, and officers were chosen. Article I of the constitution declared that purpose was to "advance the science of jurisprudence, promote the administration of justice and uniformity of legislation throughout the Union, uphold the honor of the profession of law, and encourage cordial intercourse among the members of the American bar."[p24] To achieve those goals nationally, local councils were established to encourage translating existing state bar associations from social clubs or subscription libraries into bodies patterned after the association. These were voluntary groups over which the association had no other authority than the power of suggestion.

The New Orleans Law Association was designated as the local council for Louisiana. Supposedly, Hunt, Poché, Semmes, and other like-minded members would see to the reorganization. However, progress towards that goal inched along for twenty years before it was finally reached. Why that was so can be explained in a number of ways. No doubt lingering bitterness towards anything "Northern" raised suspicions about

23 See also $_{\text{WB}}$John Austin Matzko, *Best Men of the Bar, The Early Years of the American Bar Association, 1878–1928* (Clark, 2019).

24 Carleton Hunt chaired the committee that drafted the constitution, and he also presided over the standing committee on legal education. Poché became one of the vice presidents and a member of an executive council. Semmes served on the finance committee. Their involvement can be followed in the annual reports.

the American Bar Association among some. To make the change required an alteration of the corporate charter, which the association's officers did not warm to until the 1890s. There was also the question of the priority Hunt and the others ascribed to the task. Indications are that it was not at the top of anyone's to-do list, and even if it had been they could only suggest changes because they were never officers.

Perhaps the singular explanation is bound up in Reconstruction and its unraveling. The collapse of Reconstruction and the removal of federal troops allowed former Confederate Democrats to regain control of the state's political machinery. As the reassertion of their authority gathered momentum after 1877, they rewrote the state's constitution twice, once in 1879 and again in 1898. The Constitution of 1879 set aside its predecessor that had been adopted in 1868. That constitution guaranteed full citizenship, equal access to public accommodations, public education, suffrage, and civil rights for Black people, all of which were anathema to conservative White people. Democrats excoriated it as the spawn of corrupt Republicans and undereducated Black Louisianans and clamored for a replacement. Poché and Semmes were elected to the 1879 convention, as were others in the New Orleans Law Association. All of them were determined to diminish the civil and political rights of Black people. To eliminate those rights carried the risk of contravening the Fifteenth Amendment and renewed federal intervention, so the convention moved cautiously. In the end they rewrote sections in the 1868 bill of rights. Gone were the guarantees of equal rights and free access to public places. Gone too were titles that banned discrimination in public education or the establishment of segregated schools. Despite attempts to eliminate it, the Black franchise was retained, although there were new limitations that increased the difficulties of casting a ballot.[q]

After 1877, the national government paid increasingly less heed to the fate of Black people in Louisiana and elsewhere throughout the South. Northern businessmen and attorneys were much more content to look the other way too, as they reconciled with White southerners with whom they shared similar views about the racial inferiority of Black people. Those were sentiments that New Orleans attorneys reinforced as officers and members of the ABA. This abandonment gave the Democrats chances that they did not waste. At every opportunity they used their control of the General Assembly and the courts to fix White supremacy ever more firmly in law. In 1890, the legislature, by a huge margin, passed a statute that required railway passengers to be segregated by race and travel in separate carriages.[r] The act was targeted by the Comité des Citoyens, an Afro-Creole civil rights organization, who contested the statute's legality all the way to the Supreme Court of the United States. In the case of *Plessy* v. *Ferguson* (1896), the court upheld the statute ruling that separate but equal seating on trains violated no one's rights. By extension the court's holding validated racial segregation in other public facilities, including schools, and paved the way for legal segregation in every aspect of life in Louisiana.

All that remained to finish the degradation of Black Louisianans was the elimination of their right to vote. Rather than amend the Constitution of 1879, the Democrats engineered a call for another constitutional convention. It met from February to May 1898 in Mechanics' Hall, the very site of the 1866 riot when Republicans had tried to enfranchise Black People. When the NOLA president Ernest B. Kruttschnitt opened deliberations, he described the convention as "little more than a family meeting of the Democratic Party of Louisiana."[s] It had "been called together by the people of the State to eliminate from the electorate the mass of corrupt and illiterate voters who during the past quarter century degraded our politics" (Kruttschnitt). The moment was propitious, he went on to say, because "I believe our Northern fellow-citizens begin to feel the race sympathy stilling within their breasts"(Kruttschnitt).

Furthermore, he said, northerners accepted the need to protect the "integrity of the future government of . . . Louisiana and . . . those of eight or ten other Southern States" (Kruttschnitt). So White people in the North would sympathize with "'our aspirations and efforts" to prevent "ignorant and corrupt negroes" from voting in the future (Kruttschnitt).[25]

Reducing Black suffrage was the main concern of the convention. T. F. Bell, member for Caddo Parish, chaired the suffrage and elections committee which was charged with drafting a suffrage article. Bell's committee worked for more than half the meeting before reporting back to the convention. It recommended that all voters would be required to register. In order to vote one would have to be a native-born or a naturalized resident. If he could show that he could read and write in his native tongue, he would be permitted to file his application in whatever language he was fluent. Alternatively, someone who owned or rented property assessed at three hundred dollars would also be allowed to register. Voters would have to pay a one-dollar poll tax two years before an election and would have to show their receipts on election day. A grandfather clause would exclude anyone who could not prove his grandfather or father had cast a ballot before 1867 and the advent of Reconstruction.

The convention adopted the report by a large margin, whereupon it was enacted as Article 197 of the proposed constitution.[t] When it was time for the vote on final passage, Thomas Jenkins Semmes gave a lengthy seconding speech. He forcefully praised his fellow delegates for their diligence that he said resulted in a constitution that met the present needs of the people. But he just as unashamedly reminded everyone that

25 Kruttschnitt was also chairman of the Democratic state central committee and a member of the New Orleans Law Association and the American Bar Association. For a comprehensive analysis of the convention see Michael L. Lanza, "Little More Than a Family Meeting, The Constitution of 1898," in *In Search of Fundamental Law*, 93-110.

"We met here to establish White supremacy, and the White race constitutes the Democratic party of this state."[u] It therefore followed that nothing separated "the interests of the State and those of the Democratic party"(*Journal of the Convention*, 374). His appeal to White solidarity met with thunderous applause. The speech was his last public address. A month after he spoke he died from heart failure.[u]

The suffrage article was devastatingly effective. Within two years Black voter registration declined from around 13,000 in 1898 to a mere 5,300 in 1900. White registration increased from more than 74,000 to over 125,000, and the number who qualified under the grandfather clause amounted to nearly 38,000 White men and only 111 Black men.[v]

Black people across the state and the country denounced the article, and the entire constitution, for that matter. Some wanted to mount legal challenges, but nothing happened. Contrary to the reaction of Black Americans, the Louisiana Democratic Central Committee was elated. It commissioned and circulated a pamphlet that praised it as "the greatest event in Louisiana's political history."[w]

The constitutional convention adjourned *sine die* on May 12, 1898. Three weeks later members of the New Orleans Law Association met in the Grand Opera House. An article in the New Orleans *The Daily Picayune* touted the meeting and enticed the public to attend free of charge.[x] During the course of the day-long meeting the audience listened to Henry Plauché Dart's presidential address and six other speakers.

From his address in 1898 until his death in 1934, Henry Plauché Dart was the association's dominating presence much in the same way Simeon E. Baldwin was for the American Bar Association. Both men were highly intelligent and strong-minded, but Baldwin was of a well-placed Connecticut family whereas Dart was self-fabricated. The ninth of ten siblings, Dart was born in Fort St. Philip in 1858. His mother Mary Brown Plauché Dart was a Creole, and his father Henry Dart was an English engineer who supervised construction work at the fort and sided with the Confederates. Young Dart's growing up years coincided with Reconstruction. He was emancipated when he turned eighteen because of family disagreements.[26] For a time he belonged to the White League, a Democratic, former Confederate paramilitary organization, that tried to overthrow the state government during the so-called battle of Liberty Place in 1874 and was the perpetrator of acts of violence against Black people and Republicans across the city and the state.[27] Weaned on such a strong drink, Dart developed a lifelong hatred for Black people and Republicans that led to an unyielding allegiance to White Democratic home rule. He read law and won his license when he was twenty-one. He ripened into an accomplished litigator, who over a fifty-year career would argue more than three hundred cases in the Supreme Court of Louisiana alone.

Apart from the day-to-day lawyer's work, Dart was interested in books and libraries, legal education and ethics, and better relations between the bench and bar. In furtherance of those pursuits he was inducted into the New Orleans Law Association. He was elected to the American Bar Association in 1888 and came to know Baldwin. Exposure to Baldwin's thinking and the aims of the American Bar Association shaped his ideas for transforming the New Orleans Law Association, which caused him to seek its presidency, which he won in 1898.[y]

26 Emancipation was a legal procedure whereby a minor male who was at least fifteen years old could be declared an adult. See $_{WB}$*Civil Code of the State of Louisiana* (New Orleans, 1825), 125-28.

27 For a succinct explanation of the insurrection, see Justin A. Nystrom, "The Battle of Liberty Place," *64 Parishes Online Encyclopedia.*

HENRY PLAUCHÉ DART from the Louisiana Supreme Court Portrait Collection, Law Library of Louisiana, New Orleans.

Dart's legal work eventually opened another interest: the history of Louisiana law. Out of it materialized cascades of lectures, translations of colonial judicial documents, articles, and book reviews, and those studies are now what he is best remembered for. Not only were they deeply researched, pioneering works, but they also catapulted Dart into a leading proponent of Louisiana refrains on the cultish melodies of the Lost Cause. Those riffs first appeared before the Civil War ended and were extensively tuned afterwards. Dart's unmatched command of the sources combined with polished craftsmanship that gave an unequaled authenticity to his findings. Therein lay his signal contribution to the fairy tales. He reinforced the myths of dueling Anglo and French legal cultures, the supremacy of civilian legal ways, and Lost Cause mythology with the imprimatur of flawless scholarship.[z]

After his election to the presidency of the New Orleans Law Association, Dart used the impending fiftieth anniversary of its founding to maneuver it into a professional bar society. In the run up to June 4, 1898, he called special meetings in which he received authorization to name select committees to propose the appropriate changes. There were enough votes in his pocket to assure the passage of the recommendations in principle and to leave their implementation to another special committee that he would chair.[aa] He also looked to the press for coverage to attract not only the public but potential new members.[28]

Dart's presidential address was at once retrospective and prospective. "Inasmuch as this gathering marks a new departure in the life of an old and respectable institution," he alluded to its past. Half a century had passed since the NOLA's founding and it had endured. Now it confronted a crucial moment of decision. Either it modernized or it died. Dart devoted the balance of his address to his vision of a modernized association. Once it had been possible for someone to come to the bar "without educational preparation and even win its highest accolades." Now, however it was "a self-evident truth that the candidates for admission should have a good English education and a knowledge of the languages in which the law has been written as well as a knowledge of the law and its sources."

A signature piece of Dart's thinking was the call for improved legal education. Better education undergirded the dignity of the profession. To defend "this noble edifice" against shysters, pettifoggers, and other disreputable practitioners there should be a collective effort to drive them out. Again, a modern association, Dart said, would fulfill that purpose. It would also be a means "through which to agitate . . . and to watch legislation and endeavor to shape and control it for the public good, and it should be its duty fearlessly to call attention to abuses of all kinds that may creep into the courts," and where necessary to criticize judicial rulings.

---

28 To that end the New Orleans *Daily Picayune* ran a full-page story on May 31, 1898, 21, that even included sketch portraits of Dart and other officers. Then on June 4, 10, it printed the program.

Next, Dart turned to the lack of adequate courtroom facilities. For fifty years, he noted, the civil court had sat in "a rookery which was never fitted for courthouse purposes" that was "a wretched brick barn" full of leaks and drafts. (Though he did not say so, the association's law library was housed there too.) Annually the city, he claimed, spent money on maintenance that would be better used "to begin a fine, modern courthouse." The objective of a modern association would be to convince the authorities of "the duty which they owe to this people."

Dart then remarked that the country had been at war when the association began, and so it was again. This time the fight was with Spain over Cuba. At war's end, there would be "no carpet bag government created to misrule" the Cuban people, but Louisiana lawyers "must be prepared to give the new sister that attention which we can give better than any other body of lawyers."

There was another reason for modernizing the association. The new state constitution made the city's judges elective. It was essential that they be men of integrity and learning. Such men would be impossible to elect unless the association recruited them. Collectively, members should publicly and aggressively support its chosen candidates "manfully and solely for the public good." By implication, they should stand as well. This suggestion opened the door to the association's subsequent active, behind the curtain participation in legislative and judicial politics.

Dart ended with the recommendation for a canon of ethics. He borrowed the idea from David Dudley Field, the noted New York codifier whom he knew through the American Bar Association.[cc] It consisted of eight rules that ran from obedience to the constitution and laws of the United States and those of Louisiana to defending the defenseless or the oppressed. "These simple rules of good conscience," he concluded, are the honest lawyer's eight commandments" that were the "foundations of professional ethics, and have been inherited by us along with and as heirs of all the glory of all the great lawyers of the past."[cc]

The other speakers were Henry Denis,[29] Thomas Jones Kernan,[30] William Stirling Parkerson,[31] William Wirt Howe,[32]

---

29 Henry Denis (1828–?) was born in New Orleans. His father, Henry Raphael Denis, was an attorney and his mother, Aimée Derbigny Denis, was a daughter of former governor Pierre Derbigny. Following in his father's footsteps, Denis became a lawyer. During the Civil War he fought as a Confederate private. For a time he was the official reporter of decisions for the Supreme Court of Louisiana. He taught civil law at the Tulane Law School. His book, *A Treatise on the Law of the Contract of Pledge as Governed Both by the Common Law and the Civil Law* (New Orleans, 1898), was notable at the time as the premier treatment of the subject. Alcée Fortier, *Louisiana; Comprising Sketches of Parishes, Towns, Events, Institutions, and Persons, Arranged in Cyclopedic Form* (Madison, Wisc., 1914), 3:510-11, HathiTrust.

30 Thomas Jones Kernan (1861–1911) was born in West Feliciana Parish. Like his father he became a lawyer and practiced briefly in Alabama before establishing a practice in Clinton. He partnered with Henry Plauché Dart who married his sister. A member of both the American Bar Association and the New Orleans Law Association, he was an active delegate to the constitutional convention of 1898. Obituary, New Orleans *Daily Picayune*, Jan. 10, 1911, 11.

31 William Stirling Parkerson (1857–1915) was a first-generation Louisianan whose parents had settled in St. Mary Parish in 1806. At the age of seventeen he matriculated at St. Stephan's College in New York before he returned to New Orleans to study at the University of Louisiana Law Department. He graduated as class valedictorian in 1880 and was admitted to practice. His was a New Orleans law firm. An avowed Democrat he was politically engaged though he never held office, but he belonged to the American Bar Association and the New Orleans Law Association. Fortier, *Sketches of Louisiana*, 3:346-47, 383; *Report of the Louisiana State Bar Association for 1915* (New Orleans, 1915), 151, HeinOnline.

32 Howe (1833–1909) was from upstate New York. A graduate of Hamilton College, he studied for the bar in St. Louis, Missouri, before he began to practice in New York City. He was a cavalry officer during the war, and in 1863 he opened another practice, this time in New Orleans. During Reconstruction he was chief judge of the criminal district court and a member of the Supreme Court of Louisiana. As an attorney, he represented railroads, sugar companies, and the New Orleans Board of Trade, among other corporate interests. He taught law at Columbian University in Washington, D.C., Yale College, and New York University, and he wrote widely on a variety of legal subjects and joined the ABA. George Dargo, "William Wirt Howe (1833–1909), Jurist," *American National Biography Online.*

Charles Erasmus Fenner, and William Sommer Benedict[33], who numbered among the city's silk-stocking practitioners. Denis, who taught at the Tulane Law School, spoke about the analogies and differences between civil and common law. The study of both, he observed, was necessary because both systems prevailed in Louisiana. But, in Denis's address, he was quick to claim civil law as "the fundamental law of the state." However, given the existence of the two types of law side by side and the overlap between them, he thought it appropriate to consider examples of the distinctive differences between the two. So he devoted his paper to laying the differences out. The singular example turned on his discussion of the contract of pledge about which he had recently published a widely circulated treatise.[dd]

Kernan had been an active delegate at the constitutional convention, so it was quite appropriate for him to tell his listeners about the contents of the new constitution. Showering praise on his former colleagues for their "conservatism," he pronounced them "certainly the most, careful, cautious, and conscientious body of men with which I have ever been brought into contact." He noted its main charge. That mandate had been "to disenfranchise as many negroes and as few whites as possible, without violating the prohibition of the fifteenth amendment to the Federal Constitution," and it was achieved in Article 197. The rest of what he said was a chronological summary, but he finished by observing that there were provisions pensioning "survivors of the Southern cause" and commemo-

33 Born in Alabama, William Sommer Benedict (1843–1908) was aged three when his parents removed to New Orleans where he received his secondary schooling. He clerked in a bookstore before he went into the steamboat business. When President Abraham Lincoln re-established the Federal District Court in 1863, he appointed Benedict clerk. Benedict read law with Bernard McCloskey, was admitted to the bar, and joined McCloskey's firm. A member of the New Orleans Law Association as early as 1870, he became its secretary after its reorganization in 1899 and held the post for more than a decade. "Obituary," *The Daily Picayune* (New Orleans, La.), February 2, 1908: 36.

rating "the heroic deeds of matchless valor done by them and their comrades who went down on the of battle." Henceforth, he concluded, monuments should arise to remember and "keep alive the grand, the glorious, the holy legend" of the thousands who sleep on "fame's eternal camping ground."[eeff]

Parkerson declaimed, "We are members of a learned profession, gathered together in the hope of advancing the interest of that profession; and we must be willing to expose the cancer and apply the knife." The "cancer" to which he referred was the damaged relationship between the Louisiana's bench and bar. Unnamed judges were overmighty and disrespectful of the lawyers who appeared before them. Lawyers were equally abusive and given to "irresponsible advocacy." Unless the malady was reversed, what was once a "high and honorable profession" would decay into a lowly trade and further diminish public regard for the courts, the magistracy, and the lawyers. Hence there was "now a great need of a united profession." If his listeners, "the better sort" of practitioners and judges, should return to a fellowship that worked together, and if they upheld one another, advanced legal education; and ethics, and served the public interest, then he concluded, they could do much to restore their calling to its former stature and influence, and he urged them to take up the cause.[ff]

Howe walked down memory lane regaling the audience with thumbnail drawings of attorneys he had known since his arrival in town in 1863. Even though he was a federal army officer, they came to accept him as one of their own as his career went from puppy lawyer to the presidency of the American Bar Association. He revered those men for their knowledge and commitment to "ethical practices." All of them had been an "honorable" elite who looked upon their occupation as a profession not a trade. Nevertheless, they had been mostly self-taught or otherwise informally schooled, and those means of entry were no longer suited to the complexities of the law in 1898. He uttered not a word about their bigotry or their approval of the return of White Democratic home rule, let alone their silence about the legal chicanery and the violence that brought it to pass. But then Howe accepted White supremacy as the natural order of things too.[gg]

Speaking from a former jurist's standpoint, Fenner began by saying that judges and lawyers shared a relationship in administering "the most important and far reaching of all the functions that in the organization of civil society and government are confided to officers who represent the sovereignty of the State." He observed that members of the bench and bar were one because they were all members of the same profession. As officers of the courts, judges rendered justice, and lawyers represented clients. Learned, incorruptible judges elevated the bar, whereas a "degenerate judiciary" degraded it. Therefore he exhorted the association to raise educational standards, to end "dishonorable practices, to weed out bad apples, and to raise ethical standards. If all that were done, he concluded, then "The able, learned and incorruptible men who now . . . compose the body of [Louisiana's] magistracy, will approve and encourage this association and bid it Godspeed, in the noble mission upon which it has entered."[hh]

Benedict talked about the federal district courts.[ii] Besides identifying the judges and United States attorneys and their tenures, he remarked on issues that came before those courts. One was his lengthy narrative about the 1813 fight between General Andrew Jackson and Territorial Judge Dominick Augustin Hall, and his recourse to verbatim segments of the original files laid out the controversy in some detail.[34] Another was about the restoration of the federal jurisdiction after the capture of New Orleans. In that instance he drew from his personal experience after President Lincoln named him clerk of court in 1863. A third was in relation to

34 His transcriptions, which are fully cited, make a handy collection of the pertinent original documents that are scattered throughout the federal archives or are lost.

federal involvement in the Myra Clark Gaines litigation.[35] Louisiana, he concluded, had always gained from presidential appointments who were gentlemen "versed in the practice, upright in principle, learned in the law, and esteemed by the Bar and citizens of our State, from the earliest appointments to the present day" (*Report of the Louisiana State Bar Association*). At the conclusion of Benedict's talk, everyone walked to the St. Charles Hotel for the closing banquet, which was an enormous spread of food and spirits.[36]

Although the program was akin to an American Bar Association program, it was very much grounded in the traditions of the New Orleans Law Association. Presidential addresses and lectures were familiar orations that had always been heard from the beginning. Whether earlier programs were freighted with so many long talks is uncertain because prior to 1898 the association's proceedings were neither routinely open to the public nor reported in print for distribution to the members. (Copies of any that may have been are unknown.) The Dart address and the six other speeches are unique in that respect, although one should not leap to the supposition that they were standard fare from the past. Instead, they are to be regarded for what they represented when they were delivered: the groundwork for finishing the transformation of the association from a library and dining society into a modern, professional bar organization.

---

35 Myra Clark Gaines (1806–1885) was involved in what was the longest civil suit in American history. It began in 1834 and was finally settled in her favor in 1891, six years after her death. For an overview see Katherine Jolliff Dunn, "The New Orleans woman who fought the longest legal battle in US history," *First Draft, Stories from The Historic New Orleans Collection Online*. The definitive study is Elizabeth Urban Alexander, *Notorious Woman: The Celebrated Case of Myra Clark Gaines* (Baton Rouge 2001).

36 A story in the *Daily Picayune* listed a seventh speaker, Edgar Howard Farrar (1849–1922), a prominent tax attorney who became president of the American Bar Association in 1910. See Glenn R. Conrad, "Edgar Howard Farrar," *Dictionary of Louisiana Biography Online*. However, there is no copy of his remarks in the *Proceedings of the Bar Association*, which suggests he was not present.

In the months that followed the June meeting, Dart and the other officers moved the transition along. Their first concern was for the library, which was housed in the leaky attic of the civil courts building and in desperate need of care. To obtain better accommodations they prevailed upon the city administration to allow them to use a protected storeroom in the civil courts building for their law library. Then they took out a three-thousand-dollar loan from a local bank that was spent on furnishings, shelving, and moving expenses.[jj]

While the move happened, Dart, the vice president,[37] the secretary treasurer,[38] the library chairman,[39] and one other person[40] became a special committee who drew up the replacement for the existing charter of 1855. There are no records of their deliberations, but several things seem clear. First, they turned to the constitution[41] of the American Bar Association for their model, All five belonged to the American Bar Association, so

37 I.e., Charles Ferdinand Claiborne (1848–1938) who was a grandson of Governor Claiborne. He studied at the University of Louisiana Law Department and was admitted to the bar in 1869. Active in Reconstruction politics, he belonged to the White League and like Henry Plauché Dart participated in the Battle of Liberty Place. He was on the New Orleans city council when he helped reorganize the New Orleans Law Association. Subsequently, he lost a race for mayor before he became a circuit court of appeal judge. Fortier, *Sketches of Louisiana*, 3:102-103; James D. Wilson, "William Ferdinand Claiborne," *Dictionary of Louisiana Biography Online*. Wilson misnamed this Claiborne and wrongly identified him as the former governor's son.

38 I.e., William S. Benedict.

39 I.e., Benjamin F. Forman.

40 I.e., George Denègre (1854–1930), another silk-stocking attorney, who was educated at Fordham University and the University of Louisiana Law Department. After passing his bar examination in 1878, he joined the law practice of his father-in-law T. L. Bayne and later succeeded to its head. (The firm is now known as Chaffe McCall.) He belonged to the American Bar Association and various civil and private associations in the city. George Denègre, "George Denègre," *Dictionary of Louisiana Biography Online*.

41 See Constitution, *Report of the Eleventh Annual Meeting of the American Bar Association* (Philadelphia, 1888):107-11, HeinOnline.

they would have been familiar with its charter, and they likely would have had copies on hand. Second, Dart was the primary drafter as he was the prime mover for reorganizing the New Orleans Law Association. Third, they must have taken several months to prepare the document because it was not adopted by a unanimous vote of the membership until the spring of 1899.

Nine articles comprised the new charter. Its first article styled the corporation "the Louisiana Bar Association." New Orleans was fixed as its headquarters, and it was to continue for ninety-nine years. Article II set forth the code of ethics that members were expected to uphold. It was taken word for word from Dart's presidential address. Dart's hand was also to be seen in Article III, that defined the organization's purposes with greater clarity and specificity than had the old charter. Besides its declared purpose of promoting the interests of the bar and a fraternal spirit among them, it aimed to achieve four objectives: (a.) to improve legal education; (b.) to devise rules for disciplining any attorney, whether members of the association or not, who violated the code of ethics or committed professional misdeeds; (c.) to prevail upon state and local authorities to build "a proper courthouse in the city of New Orleans; to maintain the law library; and (d.) to advance the welfare of the profession across Louisiana.[kk]

Two articles designated the officers and set up the governing structure. There would be a president, vice president, and a secretary treasurer. The president was vested with broad supervisory responsibilities. He appointed all committees and chaired them.[42] The most potent of these was an executive committee that was the center of governance. Made up of himself, the vice president, secretary-treasurer and five additional members the

42 The committees were: library, jurisprudence and law reform, international law, legal education and admission to the bar, judicial administration and reform procedures, social intercourse and annual dinner, legislation beneficial to the association, and commercial legislation. They were similar to those of the American Bar Association.

executive committee controlled "All corporate power." It was authorized to borrow funds and to issue bonds to support the library, just so long as it did not exceed the value of the collection, which was never to be moved out of New Orleans. It could enact by-laws and regulations as were needed, and it could alter or repeal of them at will. Among its other responsibilities was its control of the yearly public meeting. It chose the date and the venue at which the president was expected to deliver his annual address. It also invited "one or more gentlemen" to speak, and it was supposed to print and distribute copies of the proceedings to the membership.[ll] A by-law adopted in 1856 that had apparently divided the position of secretary treasurer into separate offices was still in effect. It was dropped in favor of a single officeholder who was both a minute taker and a financial steward. He and the other officers served one-year terms but, as in the past, the charter did not limit the number of times they might stand for reelection. Elections were to be held on the first Monday in February, although the executive committee could change the date in the event of extraordinary circumstances.[mm]

A drawn-out article detailed the criteria for membership and the costs of belonging to the association. The field of potential applicants was widened beyond Orleans Parish to include any attorney in good standing who came recommended by two members. There were three classes of members, ex officio, full, and library. Ex officio members were all the judges of the federal, state, and local courts. They paid no dues but enjoyed all the privileges of full members for as long as they were on the bench.[43] Full members had complete access to the library and could hold office or sit on committees. They were of two classes, those who resided in the New Orleans area and those who lived elsewhere. Anyone who just

43 Because the records of earlier meetings are lost, it is impossible to determine if this was a new category or merely a continuance of one that had come into being at some time before 1899.

wanted access to the library was classed a library member. An elaborate vetting process preceded an invitation to join. Invitees were expected to pay an initial fee and annual dues up front, and they or other members were dropped if they were delinquent.[nn]

Article VII established the disposition complaints of professional misconduct. When charges were lodged against association members the accuser filed the particulars in writing with the president. The executive committee investigated. If it decided that there was a case, then it convened a five-member court to adjudicate it, and the punishment ranged from a reprimand, a suspension, or a recommendation for disbarment. When an offender did not belong to the association, the executive committee was empowered to investigate and to pass its findings to outside authorities. The latter claim was an opening to the day when the association might actually exercise disciplinary power over all attorneys statewide. It would become a source of hostility that nonmembers harbored well into the twentieth century. The two remaining articles repealed the old charter and provided for amending this one.

As required by law, the signed original was presented to the Orleans Parish district attorney Robert H. Marr. Marr reviewed it to certify whether it complied with all the applicable statutes. He determined it did. It was filed in the recorder of mortgages' office, and with that the migration of the New Orleans Law Association to the Louisiana Bar Association was finally accomplished.[oo]

NOTES

a. Lawrence L. Hewitt, "David Glasgow Farragut (05 July 1801–11 August 1870)," *American National Biography Online.*

b. G. Howard Hunter, "Fall of New Orleans and Federal Occupation," 64 Parishes Encyclopedia Online.

c. Hans L. Trefousse, "Benjamin Franklin Butler (05 November 1818–11 January 1893)," *American National Biography Online.*

d. "Proclamation, May 1, 1862" in *The War of the Rebellion: A compilation of the Official Records of the Union and Confederate Armies*, comp. Robert N. Scott, et al. (Washington, D.C., 1880-1901), 1, no. 6: 719.

e. Thomas W. Helis, "Of Generals and Jurists, The Judicial System Under Union Occupation, May 1862–April 1865," in *A Law Unto Itself*, Billings and Fernandez, 128-37.

f. Kathryn Page, "A First Born Child of Liberty: The Constitution of 1864," in $_{WB}$*In Search of Fundamental Law: Louisiana's Constitutions, 1812-1974*, ed. Warren M. Billings and Edward F. Haas (Baton Rouge, 1993), 52-68. See also Justin A. Nystrom, "Reconstruction," 64 Parishes Encyclopedia Online.

g. La. CONST. of 1868, HeinOnline; Charles Vincent, "Black Constitution Makers: The Constitution of 1868," in *In Search of Fundamental Law*, 69-80.

h. "Membership Roster," in *Proceedings of the Louisiana State Bar Association, 1898–1902*, (New Orleans, 1870), 1: 18, HeinOnline; $_{WB}$Warren M. Billings, ed., *The Historic Rules of the Supreme Court of Louisiana, 1813–1879* (University of Southwestern Louisiana), 30-31.

i. Henry Plauché Dart, "The History of the Supreme Court of Louisiana," in *Louisiana Reports* (1913), iii.

j. James D. Wilson, "Felix Pierre Poché," *Dictionary of Louisiana Biography Online*: Louisiana Historical Association.

k. Carolyn E. De Latte, "Carleton Hunt," *American National Biography Online*; "Obituary," *The Times-Picayune* (New Orleans, La.), August 1921; Louisiana Digital Library.

l. Marcus Carriere Jr., "Thomas Jenkins Semmes," *Dictionary of Louisiana Biography Online*: Louisiana Historical Association; "Obituary," *The Times-Picayune* (New Orleans, La.), June 1899.

m. "Summary of Events." *American Law Review*, 5 (1871): 556, HathiTrust.

n. Charles C. Goetsch, "Simeon Eben Baldwin (05 February 1840–30 January 1927)," *American National Biography Online.*

o. Simeon E. Baldwin, "Founding of the American Bar Association," *American Bar Association Journal*, 3, (1917): 658, HathiTrust; Louisiana Digital Library.

p. La. Ann. of the American Bar Association (1878), 1: 30, HeinOnline.

q. Ronald M. Labbé, "That the Reign of Robbery Will Never Return to Louisiana: The Constitution of 1879," in *In Search of Fundamental Law*, 81-93.

r. "An Act to Promote the Comfort of Passengers on Railway Trains . . . and to Repeal All Laws and Parts of Laws Contrary to or Inconsistent with the Provisions of this Act," La. In *Acts of Louisiana, 1890*: 152-54, HeinOnline.

s. Ernest B. Kruttschnitt, speech, (February 8, 1898) in *Official Journal of the Proceedings of the Constitutional Convention of the State of Louisiana* (New Orleans, 1898): 8-9, 9-10, HathiTrust.

t. Michael L. Lanza, "Little More Than a Family Meeting, The Constitution of 1898," in *In Search of Fundamental* Law, 99-103; "Constitution of the State of State of Louisiana Adopted in Convention at the City of New Orleans, May 12, 1898," HeinOnline (1898): 77-80.

u. *Journal of the Convention*, 374.

v. Lanza, "Little More Than a Family Meeting," 105; George E. Cunningham, "Constitutional Disenfranchisement of the Negro in Louisiana, 1898." *Negro History Bulletin*, 29 (1966): 147-48, 158-60, 166, 174, 184.

w. Cunningham, "Constitutional Disenfranchisement," 103-104; *The Convention of '98. A Complete Work on the Greatest Political Event in Louisiana's Political History, And a Sketch of the Men Who Composed It*, Hathi Trust (New Orleans, 1898).

x. *The Times-Picayune* (New Orleans, La.), June 4, 1898: 30.

y. Marie E. Windell, "Henry Plauché Dart," *Dictionary of Louisiana Biography Online*: Louisiana Historical Association; ABA. Ann. 11 (1888): 101, HeinOnline; Justin A. Nystrom, "White League," 64 Parishes Encyclopedia Online; ABA. Ann. 21 (1898): 722, HeinOnline.

z. Warren M. Billings, "Mixed Jurisdictions and Convergence, The Louisiana Example," in $_{WB}$*Magistrates and Pioneers: Essays in the History of American Law*, ed. Warren M. Billings, (Clark, 2011), 364-68.

aa. *The Times-Picayune* (New Orleans, La.), May 4, 1898: 8; *The Times-Picayune* (New Orleans), La.), May 31, 1898: 5.

bb. James R. Maxeiner, "David Dudley Field (13 February 1805–1894)," *American National Biography Online.*

cc. *Proceedings of the Louisiana State Bar Association*, 1898, HeinOnline: 33-40.

dd. *Report of the Louisiana State Bar Association*, 1898, HeinOnline: 41-54.

ee. *Report of the Louisiana State Bar Association*, HienOnline: 56-58, 72, 73.

ff. *Report of the Louisiana State Bar Association*, HienOnline: 73-84.

gg. *Report of the Louisiana State Bar Association*, HeinOnline: 84-99.

hh. *Report of the Louisiana State Bar Association*, HeinOnline: 99-108.

ii. *Report of the Louisiana State Bar Association*, HeinOnline: 108-44. There is an appendix in the *Report of the Louisiana State Bar Association*, that lists the judges and U.S. attorneys.

jj. *The Times-Picayune* (New Orleans, La.), August 9, 1898: 3; Henry Plauché Dart, "Presidential Address," (May 12, 1899) in *Report of the Louisiana State Bar Association*, 1:152, HeinOnline.

kk. "Charter of 1899," in *Proceedings of the Louisiana State Bar Association, 1899* (New Orleans, 1899): 20-21, HeinOnline.

ll. *Proceedings of the Louisiana State Bar Association*: 22.

mm. "By-Laws," in *Proceedings of the Louisiana State Bar Association*: 17; "Charter of 1899," in *Proceedings of the Louisiana State Bar Association*: 23.

nn. "Charter of 1899" in *Proceedings of the Louisiana State Bar Association*: 23-25.

oo."Charter of 1899" in *Proceedings of the Louisiana State Bar Association*: 26-27.

Chapter Four

The Bar Association at Work

In 1899, shifts were stirring in the Louisiana economy, politics, and social fabric. The changes they unleashed invested Louisiana with a turbulence that would epitomize it down to the 1930s and beyond. Industry lured people away from the land. Ruthless exploitation of natural resources and domination of the transportation networks enabled giant corporations to control most of the new economy. Automobiles, paved highways, and bridges changed the look of Louisiana forever. Motion pictures and radio opened exciting new avenues for communication and entertainment. Mass advertising encouraged consumerism on a scale unforeseen heretofore. These novelties lessened Louisianans' isolation from other parts of the country, but they hardly altered the contemporary social fabric. Louisianans were still desperately poor, astonishingly uneducated, and rigidly segregated. Politically, the White only Democratic Party ruled supreme. Its leaders imbibed just enough of the reforms touted by the national Progressive Movement to impose a type of modest uplift that held restive Louisianans in check. There were new fields of law. The more obvious ones were social legislation, tax law, labor law, workmen's compensation, and mineral law. Their emergence added to the volume of appeals that went up to the Supreme Court, which fostered a situation similar to that of the 1830s. Cumulatively, these changes infused the era of Huey P. Long and abetted the near destruction of the bar association.[a]

* * *

There was nothing inevitable about what would become of the reinvented bar association. It could have withered away. It didn't. Instead, it sustained itself and reached for goals that Henry Plauché Dart wrote in the 1899 charter. Chief among those ends was fashioning the Louisiana Bar Association (LBA) into a voluntary society that defined lawyering and brought certain attorneys from across Louisiana into its company. Promoting the construction of a new courthouse and extending the association's influence beyond New Orleans were means to that objective.

In 1902 Dart, Bernard McCloskey, Ernest B. Kruttschnitt, and William P. Ball persuaded the General Assembly to establish a new courthouse in New Orleans. The statute called for a five-man commission to oversee the project but said nothing about housing the bar association and the library, which was another of Dart's aims. An appropriation of 200,000 dollars from the state and 375,000 dollars from the city went to the commissioners, who were named by the governor and the mayor.[b]

Meeting for the first time in October 1902, the commissioners elected McCloskey president, Kruttschnitt vice president, and Ball secretary-treasurer. George H. Dunbar and J. Davidson Hill rounded out the commission.[c44] Finding a site proved to be as time consuming as it was complicated. A preferred location on Lafayette Square was precluded because the federal government preempted it for a courthouse/post office building. Sites on the Uptown side of Canal Street were either too pricey or they provoked the opposition of nearby residents. J. A. Mercier and some other French Quarter residents proposed building on a tract bounded by Conti, Chartres, St.

44 Ball resigned shortly after his appointment, and he was replaced by Arthur McGuirk who served until the commission was dissolved. Aristide Hopkins, George Lanaux, Charles T. Soniat, and Dart were later commissioners.

Louis, and Royal streets. They had obtained options on the property for only a third over its total assessed value. They offered it together with pledges from the neighboring locals and future sales of the demolished building materials from the site. The commissioners accepted Mercier's proposal, exercised the options and purchased the site for 203,973.29 dollars. Then, in 1904, they persuaded the General Assembly to allow the city to issue 750,000 dollars' worth of bonds, and their sale combined with state appropriations and private donations would put the project on stable financial footings.[d]

The project nearly came to grief after a group of city taxpayers raised objections that they took to the Supreme Court. The group of taxpayers argued that it was invalid and unconstitutional because the General Assembly had exceeded its constitutional powers and the project should be abandoned. In the spring of 1905, the Court ruled in their favor, and it seemed as though that was the end of a new courthouse. The city attorney, his deputy, and the attorney general petitioned for a rehearing knowing full well that even if it were granted it would be difficult to persuade the justices to reverse themselves. Consequently, they looked to Ernest Kruttschnitt to prepare their petition. Kruttschnitt was a compelling choice. An enthusiastic backer of the project, he had lobbied for it, and he had assisted in drafting its enabling legislation. But most importantly, he had chaired the constitutional convention of 1898 so he knew more about the constitution than anyone else. His brief was persuasive, and in the fall of 1905, the Court reversed itself and declared the project valid and constitutional.[e45]

Once the legal position was no longer suspect, and the financing was secure, the commission began its search for an

---

45 William S. Benedict, Ernest T. Florance, and William O. Hart initiated the suit. City attorney Samuel L. Gilmore, assistant city attorney Henry Garland Dupré, and Attorney general Walter Guion filed for the rehearing. Kruttschnitt was of counsel for them. He died in April 1906. See Benedict et al. v. the City of New Orleans et al., *Louisiana Reports*, 115 (1905): 645-68.

architect to design the building and a general contractor to put it up. They engaged two local architects, Thomas Sully and William H. Freret, as unpaid consultants to advise them on the way to identify both. Sully and Freret advised holding national competitions with the winners receiving 5,000-dollar prizes for their entries. A design submitted by Frederick and Ten Eyck Brown of Brown, Brown, and Marye of Atlanta took the architectural prize, and A. B. Stanard of New York City won as the general contractor.[f]

The Browns designed the courthouse in what is now called the Beaux Arts style. It was out of scale with its surroundings though its massive size equaled the largest public buildings in the country, containing as it did about 160,000 square feet of usable space on four floors and a basement. The structure was of reinforced concrete, which was thought to guard against fires. Georgia marble faced the first two stories while terra-cotta clad the upper stories. Ample natural lighting would come from 360 windows. Negotiations about these and the other types and sources of building materials, as well as the design and utilization of interior spaces, and whom to employ as subcontractors went on for months before all the details were agreed.[46]

Construction began in March 1907. Nine months later the commissioners organized a cornerstone laying ceremony that coincided with the anniversary of the Battle of New Orleans. Royal Street from Canal to below St. Louis was bedecked with flags, bunting, and other festive decorations. Attended by a large crowd of ordinary citizens, public officials, and foreign consuls, the celebration began with an invocation by Reverend Wallace T. Palmer, a Protestant minister. Governor Newton D. Blanchard, Chief Justice Joseph Breaux, Mayor Martin Behrmann, and Bernard McCloskey spoke ahead of Henry Plauché Dart who delivered the principal address. Retelling the history of earlier

46 The negotiations are detailed in the Courthouse Commission Minute Book, 158-300.

courthouses, he lamented their abandonment, but he said they had always been unsuitable, and now the courts were soon to be housed in a magnificent new temple of justice. After Archbishop James Blenk gave the benediction, the Washington Artillery fired a salute, and the ceremony concluded with music from William J. Braun's Naval Reserve Concert Band.[g]

On October 1, 1910, the building was ready for occupancy. The Supreme Court, Court of Appeal, Civil District Court, city courts, attorney general, state law library, civil sheriff's office, constables' office, recorder of mortgages, and conveyance office moved in. And just as Dart had always intended, so did the Louisiana Bar Association. Situated on the third floor, there was rent free permanent space for the association's corporate offices, committee meetings, and the library.[47]

The librarian outfitted the rooms that received the collection. A New Orleanian, Stephen A. Mascaro (1877–1965), was a pioneer among Louisiana's professional law librarians. His interest in books traced to his exposure to them as an eleven-year-old lad while he was an office boy in a law office. Self-taught, he began his career when he modernized the Civil District Court collection into an orderly library that he updated regularly. At first he met resistance from the judges and the lawyers who were averse to his changes, but they eventually came to appreciate his innovations.

Hired by the LBA in 1907, Mascaro stayed for the next thirty-seven years. He wrote the rules that governed the use of the

47 In July 1910 the General Assembly dissolved the building commission and gave custody of the courthouse to a management commission. It put the day to day supervision and care of the building in the hands of a superintendent/secretary. See Act No. 244, "An Act To create a Commission which will have custody and control of the new Court House in the City of New Orleans . . .," *Acts of Louisiana, 1910*, 408-10, HeinOnline. The first superintendent was a small- time criminal lawyer called Edwin I. Mahoney whose granddaughter Ruth Mahoney was on the staff of the Law Library of Louisiana from 1987 to 2021. See Miriam Childs, "Ruth Mahoney: Long-time Library Associate Retires," *De Novo*, 18 (Spring/Summer 2021), 3 and Ruth Mahoney, "Spotlight on Edward I. Mahoney," ibid., 8 (Summer/Fall, 2010), 3.

library. They were intended to provide a comfortable workplace and ready access to the books.[48] If needed, patrons could seek his assistance or avail themselves of paper, pencils, pens, and ink that were available for the asking. He cataloged the collection according to a system that he designed. (It was akin to the one employed by the United States Department of Justice.)[49] His supervisors chaired the one-man library committee, and they relied on him to identify holes in the collection and to recommend new titles they needed to add. Their close collaboration not only filled the gaps, it increased the scope and size of the collection. Among the additions were up-to-date holdings in French and other civilian sources that strengthened those areas of the collection. He augmented the number of bar journals, federal and state statutes, case reporters, and a newer class of literature, the university-based law review. Such was the pace of the additions that within five years of Mascaro's appointment the collection approached twelve thousand volumes. Mascaro more than trebled that number over the next two decades, and when the library was dispersed in the 1930s, it was one of the largest, most comprehensive law libraries in Louisiana. After that, Mascaro retained the title of librarian and remained assistant secretary-treasurer of the LBA until he retired in 1961.[50]

---

48 Those rules and other regulations were codified in article VII of the revised Charter of 1912.

49 In 1911 Mascaro gave an inscribed copy of his first catalog to the University of Michigan Law Library, which is accessible via Google Books. In addition to the preface, which explained his cataloging system, were a roster of the association's officers, an illustration of the stacks and the rules of the library.

50 The LBA had to borrow five thousand dollars to cover furnishings and moving expenses. See Charles Rosen, Report of Library Committee, May 2, 1910, *Annual Report of the Louisiana Bar Association, 1910*, 117-18, HeinOnline. The latest additions to the collection appear in the annual reports of the LBA. Mascaro prepared printed copies of the library catalog that he gave to members. On Mascaro see, New Orleans *Times-Picayune*, Dec. 14, 1965, 3. On the volume count see *Law Library Journal*, 1 (1912): 40.

Not only had his stewardship raised the quality of the collection, it also enhanced the value of the library for members.

A composite profile of the members depicts who these lawyers were. Collectively, they were an elite band who lived and worked in Louisiana's urban centers. Individually, some were the sons or grandsons of old-line legal families. Others had married into wealth and position. The immigrants from other states and abroad had risen above their origins by dint of cleverness and luck. Related to one another, all belonged to the same sets of social clubs and civic societies. They segregated along class and racial divides, and they regarded the world, their place in it, and White supremacy as the natural order of the universe. Although some had read for the bar, most had obtained law degrees either from the law schools at Harvard, Yale, University of Virginia, and Washington & Lee or from Tulane, Louisiana State, and Loyola universities.

Conservative to the core, the members were established fixtures in Democratic political circles and officeholders in local and state government. They had ties to the judiciary, and not a few were close to justices of the Supreme Court of Louisiana. Their links to the American Bar Association (ABA), the American Judicature Society (AJS), the American Law Institute, the Association of American Law Schools, the American Legion, the Veterans of Foreign Wars, and other national organizations joined them in communion with like-minded attorneys across the nation. Instead of working solo, they were partners in law firms, and in the smaller cities they were usually the largest or the only firms in town.

No matter the geographic locations, those partnerships were extraordinarily lucrative, given that they represented the monopolies that controlled so much of the state's economy. The members avoided cases from the generality of Louisianans because there was little profit in them and because the legal needs of the lower classes ran counter to the interests of their corporate clients. Not unexpectedly, their contempt aroused fierce animosity from lower class people and rural, less educated lawyers who despised them.

The effort to recruit such lawyers paralleled the courthouse project. Any attorney "in good standing," including women, could be recommended for membership[h]. Of the 151 lawyers who were dues-paying members in 1902 only 7 percent hailed from outside New Orleans.[51] There were 364 members by 1910, of whom 159, or 43 percent, were country lawyers. For the first time in 1922 there were more small town lawyers than New Orleanians, and the small town lawyers constituted the majority into the 1930s.[52] In spite of the steady growth, the sum of outsiders and New Orleanians never equaled more than a third of Louisiana's active attorneys (La. Ann. 1929).[53]

Nonetheless, outward expansion influenced who led the LBA and how it conducted its business. It opened the leadership to outsiders who began to fill committees and elective offices. In 1909, Edward Hughes Randolph, a member from Shreveport, was the first of five outsiders to be elected the president, but a decade passed before another one, Charles A. McCoy of Lake Charles, rose to the presidency. He was followed by Fred G. Hudson Jr. of Monroe (1922), Sidney L. Herold of Shreveport (1927), and Cecil Charles Bird Jr. of Baton Rouge (1930). A modification of the vice presidency created more openings. The office was expanded from one to a vice president from the state's supreme court districts, and they were charged with vetting potential members and bringing issues of local concern to the Executive Committee and the annual meeting.[i] More opportunities opened to the general membership after the president was authorized to appoint specific standing com-

51 Individuals who belonged to the association and were elevated to the federal or state judiciaries were reckoned ex officio members as long as they held office. For most of the years before the charter revision of 1929, they were inactive.

52 I compiled these data from the membership rolls in the *Annual Reports*.

53 In 1929 Walker B. Spencer estimated the total number at 1,500.

mittees to assist in furthering the LBA's business. One concentrated on affiliating with local bar associations and seeding new ones. Three focused on law reform, legal education, bar admissions, and ethics. Another coordinated with the American Bar Association to promote uniform state laws. The library committee managed the library, and a committee on publications prepared the *Annual Reports* that included the committee on obituaries' yearly record of members' deaths.[j] The committees worked with the Executive Committee in the intervals between annual meetings and drew up the reports that were presented to the annual meetings and printed in the *Annual Reports*.

It was the prerogative of the president and the Executive Committee to set a date and an agenda for annual meetings. Customarily, they chose dates that preceded when the General Assembly went into session, so they picked days in April or May. The choice ensured their having in hand the draft bills that the association lobbied the legislators to enact. They decided where to meet and for how long. Spreading outward from New Orleans prompted their decision in 1907 to hold two-day conferences. Starting with Shreveport, those meetings rotated between Alexandria, Baton Rouge, Lafayette, Lake Charles, New Orleans, Monroe, and Opelousas. One two-day conference even met on the Mississippi Gulf Coast, and another was held with the Texas Bar Association in Texarkana, Texas.

The agenda conformed to a set pattern. Meetings ordinarily began early in the morning on the first day with the call to order. The mayor of the host town, or his designee, and someone from the local bar, greeted the delegates and were thanked by the president for their hospitality. Those speeches were invariably florid and long. The secretary-treasurer and the committee chairmen gave their reports and responded to questions from the floor before the reports were received and filed. After lunch, invited guests spoke at the convention. Those speakers might be a member, a judge, a law dean, a political figure, or someone from a national association such as the American

Bar Association or the American Judicature Society. Their talks ran the gamut from the historical to the need for reforms to the judiciary.[54] Time was allotted for informal discussions of their remarks, committee recommendations, and other matters before the afternoon session ended. Then everyone dined at the annual banquet. The meal and the quantity of spirits were enormous.[55] After dinner toasts lasted well into the night, so it was a testament to the stamina of the delegates who showed up at mid-morning on the second day. Sleepy-eyed and hung over they answered the roll call and listened to the presidential address. It was a summary of the association's previous year's activities and a commentary on recent issues of interest to the membership. Miscellaneous business was considered before the election of officers from a slate chosen by the president. The new officers were installed, and the meeting adjourned.[56]

Changing the law, legal education, bar admissions, and ethics were subjects that were discussed at nearly every annual meeting after 1899. Regarding the law, the discussions revolved around the ways and means to revise the statutes; the civil code; and the jurisdiction, size, and number of courts. Debating standards of legal education turned on defining the nature of lawyering and who was worthy to become an attorney. Worthiness depended upon improving the association's role in educating and vetting applicants and binding *all* lawyers to its standards of ethical behavior. Charles E. Fenner, William O. Hart, Edwin T. Merrick Jr., and Walker B. Spencer stand out as major influences among all the members who fostered those issues. Until they died, they steered the associ-

54 For a list of speakers and the titles of their addresses, see *Report, 1934–1941*, 258-62, HeinOnline.

55 For example, see the menu for 1905 and an example of the toasts, see *Annual Reports, 1905*; *1910*, 39-41; 163-79, HeinOnline.

56 This paragraph is based on the proceedings of the meeting at Lafayette in 1929. See the *Annual Report*, 3-162, HeinOnline.

ation towards those ends albeit with mixed results in convincing lawyers, judges, legislators, and voters to comport with its point of view. They are also suggestive of why that vision was an object of scorn by the body politic.

CHARLES ERASMUS FENNER *from the Louisiana Supreme Court Portrait Collection, Law Library of Louisiana, New Orleans.*

Born in Tennessee, Fenner (1834–1911) was the only child of Dr. Erasmus Fenner who moved the family to New Orleans in the 1840s. Charles E. Fenner received his secondary schooling in New Orleans, graduated the Western Military Institute, and attended the University of Virginia before he matriculated at the University of Louisiana Law Department. Admitted to the bar in 1855, he was a prosperous lawyer before he fought as a Confederate artilleryman throughout the war and rejoined his law firm. Afterwards he joined Confederate veterans' organizations, and as president of the R. E. Lee Memorial Association, he delivered the principal address at the unveiling of the Lee monument on Tivoli Circle in New Orleans. Following a term in the

General Assembly of 1866 he refused to run for elective office ever again. Instead, he concentrated on teaching, writing, and the development of Tulane University. Governor Louis A Wiltz appointed him to a four-year term on the Supreme Court in 1890; four years later the governor reappointed him. However the discovery that being simultaneously a professor in civil law at Tulane and president of the Tulane Board of Administrators was prohibited by a state statute compelled him to leave the Supreme Court in 1894.[k]

His colleagues reckoned Fenner an able jurist who crafted clear, well-reasoned opinions, and they especially applauded his decision in the state portion of a case that went to the Supreme Court of the United States. Speaking for his court in 1892, Fenner upheld a statute that required railway passengers to be segregated by race and to travel in separate carriages.[l] He ruled that just so long as the accommodations were equivalent, separating Louisianans by race in public conveyances neither discriminated against nor deprived anyone of their right to equal protection under the Fourteenth Amendment. In *Plessy v. Ferguson* (1896) the high court in Washington, D.C. refused to overrule him, and its refusal embedded the doctrine of separate but equal race relations in the law of the land.[57]

Fenner and Henry Plauché Dart were of like minds about the state and condition of the bar. That similarity explains his support for chartering the Louisiana Bar Association and why Dart was able to recruit him as one of the six speakers at the final annual meeting of the New Orleans Law Association (NOLA). His influence in the untried organization during its first decade was primarily on its views about legal education.

Hart (1857–1929) was born in New Orleans and received his secondary education at Clark's School and Lusher's Academy.

57 A printed text of Fenner's decision is in Philip B. Kurland and Gerhard Casper, eds. *Landmark Briefs and Arguments of the Supreme Court of the United States: Constitutional Law*, 80 vols. (Arlington, Va., 1975), 13:123-34.

Instead of attending university, he read law before he passed the bar. A partner in the firm of Braughn, Buck & Dinkelspiel, he remained in the partnership until it dissolved some years before his death. Locally, he joined the LBA and the NOLA, and he was a twenty-five-year appointee to the National Conference of Commissioners on Uniform State Law. Nationally, among others, he belonged to the American Bar Association, the Commercial Law League of America, the American Society of International Law, the International Law Association, the American Institute of Criminal Law and Criminology, the American Judicature Society, and the Maritime Law Association of the United States, and he was a recognized leader in those organizations. He was once treasurer of the Louisiana Historical Society and twice commandant of Camp Beauregard, Sons of Confederate Veterans. Three times a member of the state bar examining committee, he also lectured at the Louisiana State University and Tulane law schools.[m]

Like every other attorney who practiced commercial law, Hart faced the time-consuming annoyances of navigating his way through a jungle of statutes, a maze of court rules, and a thicket of courts. His frustrations developed into an interest in efficient state governance, and he sought ways to achieve it. A close student of the 1870 civil code, he participated in a failed effort to modernize the code. Reform through uniform state law was an approach he mastered after he was named to the National Conference of Commissioners on Uniform State Law. Respect for his legal scholarship gained him a seat in the General Assembly that wrote and enacted the Constitution of 1913. Hart favored changes that would have stripped it of statutory detail and modernized the executive, legislative, and judicial branches, but they were turned aside. He urged the constitutional convention of 1921 to adopt similar revisions, but they were ignored. However it was his career-long commitment to adapting the theories of the National Uniform State Law Movement in Louisiana that contributed his influence on the LBA. For years, Hart was either a member or chairman of the standing committee on uniform state law where he was a persistent advocate of those principles. He drafted bills that were submitted to the General Assembly; several became law, but the legislators were slow to embrace his ideas.[n]

Merrick (1859–1935) graduated from Vanderbilt University and read law with his namesake, the former Confederate chief justice of Louisiana.[o] He was inducted into the New Orleans Law Association and held memberships in the New Orleans Bar Association, the American Bar Association, the Louisiana Bar Association, and the Illinois State Bar Association. Unlike his father, he generally avoided the public sphere, preferring instead to devote himself to his practice, writing, and the bar. His firm, Merrick & Schwartz, represented businesses such as the Chicago meat packers Armour & Company; the Canal Commercial Trust & Savings Bank;, the music publisher and instrument retailer, Philip Werlein, Ltd.; the financiers Newman-Saunders & Company; and the New Orleans Clearinghouse.[58] He wrote on a variety of legal topics that appeared in newspapers and law reviews, and his books were his editions of the 1870 civil code, which appeared in 1900, 1913, and 1925.[59]

The 1899 edition was something of an homage to his father, who had nearly finished an updated version of the code just before he died. Merrick designed the book "for the practical use of a lawyer," and it was based on accumulated notes rather than collections of decisions.[p] The annotations were his, although he used older references from his father's copy of the code that the

58 Clearing houses were a national network of holding companies for banks. They facilitated banks in adjusting and paying daily balances that were due to and received from one another at one time and in one place on each day. See James G. Cannon, *Clearing-Houses, Their History and Administration* (New York, 1900), HathiTrust.

59 For example, see Edwin T. Merrick, "Recent Interpretation of the Uniform Warehouse Receipt Law," *Southern Law Quarterly*, 1 (1916): 199-208, HeinOnline.

Chief Justice made throughout his career at the bar and on the bench. Merrick hoped "my book may prove of practical value to the profession and give some evidence of the labor and time spent upon it" (Merrick, preface). His hope proved prophetic. The book's popularity and the respect for his achievement led to the second and third editions. Perhaps he cast a cold eye on attempts to overhaul the code because they would break a cherished link with his late father (Merrick, preface).

When it came to his bar activities, Merrick had more pies than fingers. He was a consultant to the federal courts in New Orleans. For nearly the first quarter of the twentieth century, he chaired the state bar examination committee and routinely recommended improvements that the Supreme Court of Louisiana approved. He not only supported the Tulane Law School when it launched its law review, but also acted as an advisor to the student editors and underwrote some of the publishing expenses. But his biggest pie was his work with the LBA. His influence was twofold. Longevity ranked him apart, and his steadfast presence was a source of continuity. The presidency and seats in all the other offices and committees allowed Merrick numerous opportunities to fashion bills that the association recommended to the General Assembly. Foremost among them were bills that would raise the educational and ethical standards of the bar, and he made general arguments for them in his two presidential addresses.[q]

Walker B. Spencer (1868–1941) grew up in New Orleans.[r] His father was a one-time associate supreme court judge, so it was natural for him to follow the law, but before he passed the bar he spent several years on the editorial staff of the *The Baton Rouge Advocate*. After finishing his studies at Tulane and the University of Virginia, he was admitted to practice. He joined the LBA, NOLA, ABA, AJS, Bar Association of the City of New York, and other societies. Retired Justice Charles E. Fenner and he were partners until 1894 when he entered the firm of Howe, Spencer, and Cocke, which afterwards reemerged as Spencer, Phelps, Dunbar, and Marx.[60] As an active attorney, he daily confronted the same creaky, antiquated courts, procedures, and laws that bedeviled Hart and Merrick. Those inadequacies were constant reminders of what he believed was a pressing need for reforms if Louisiana's legal order was ever to be modernized, and he devoted much of his career to attaining those changes. He rewrote a city charter for New Orleans and helped to draft the statutes that instituted the Australian system of balloting in local and state elections. At the Constitutional Convention of 1898, he assisted with drafting the restrictive suffrage article. He collaborated with the General Assembly on a revised civil practice statute and drew the first law that governed the organization of corporations. Inarguably, he was at his most influential when the LBA considered reforming the legislature and the judiciary.

Curtailing the huge number of statutes enacted by the General Assembly was much discussed at the New Iberia meeting in 1915, and that discussion was an opportunity for Spencer. He argued that existing legislative procedures caused all those numerous "hasty and ill-conceived" laws and they should be revised.[s] To that end, he moved the appointment of a special committee that would formulate those revisions and others "relating to Judicial Reform and other matters heretofore or at this meeting approved by this association" (Deacon, 83). Opinions were sharply divided in the ensuing discussion, but with some minor changes to the resolution, it passed. After the meeting President Benjamin Wall Kernan named the special committee; it consisted of twenty-five members of whom fifteen were New Orleanians, including Spencer who chaired it.[t][61]

Spencer wrote the committee's report and presented it at the 1916 annual meeting. He drew ideas not only from

60 Phelps was Esmond Phelps who was the president of the association in 1926. Dunbar was Charles E. Dunbar, Jr., who held the presidency in 1931. Marx was Frederic C. Marx, a New Orleans lawyer and long-time member of the association.

61 The committee list is in *Annual Report, 1916*, 4-5, HeinOnline.

national Progressive reformers, he also scoured the *Annual Reports* for inspiration.[62] Comprised of two articles, Part A proposed reforms to proceedings in the General Assembly. Article I provided for biennial sessions divided into two meetings that would sit respectively for fifteen and forty-five days. The business of the first meeting was only for the purpose of organizing each house and determining which bills to accept that were introduced by the members or various interest groups such as the association. At the end of the fifteen days, the Assembly adjourned for an additional thirty days before it reconvened for its second meeting. In the interval the secretary of state was required to print the accepted bills in a pamphlet that went to all state executive officers, senators, representatives, judges of courts of record, mayors, police jury presidents, public and law libraries, and to any private citizen who paid for a copy. The second meeting dealt only with those bills that were introduced at the first meeting and there were definitions of committee powers and restrictions on how amendments could be made. Article II described the governor's role. Any legislation he initialed was law; any he vetoed became law if he was overridden by a two-thirds majority of both houses.[u]

Part B was Spencer's scheme for a revising of the judiciary, and it was made up of thirty articles.[v] Besides the Supreme Court, there would be four courts of appeal and four district courts, the latter being drawn from the state's four judicial districts. The Supreme Court would consist of seven justices. He who sat longest was chief. They all had to retire when they turned seventy and were entitled to pensions that might equal their full salaries. There would be three judges for each circuit court and as

62 See for examples, the discussion of two draft bills to reform appellate procedures from 1910 that were defeated, *Annual Report, 1910*, 19-93, HeinOnline; discussion of three draft bills that were forwarded to the General Assembly from 1911, *Annual Report, 1911*, 98-136, HeinOnline; discussion of whether to seek repeal of act, 68-69; discussion about the size of the Supreme Court and whether the justices should continue to rule on issues of law and fact, *Annual Report, 1915*, 23ff, HeinOnline.

many as eight for each district court, and their terms would be eight, and four years respectively. Except for the first (Orleans, St. John the Baptist, St. Charles, St. Bernard, Plaquemines, and Jefferson parishes) no two members of any court could reside in the same judicial district. All judges were required to meet the same educational and experiential requirements that were specified in earlier constitutions. They held their places during good behavior and were subject to impeachment and removal, which also kept faith with previous constitutional mandates.

No fan of electing judges, Spencer returned the appointing power to the governor, but with this wrinkle. At the general election that was nearest to the expiration of an incumbent's term the voters could decide this ballot question. The ballot read as though: "(name of Judge) has served continuously for . . . (number of years) years as . . . (position occupied) of the. . . (name of Court) Court. Shall he be continued in office?" If the vote was "no," then he was dismissed, and the governor named his replacement.[w]

Spencer went a considerable distance in redefining the courts' jurisdictions and their exercise. Under Appendix B, the Supreme Court supervised the lower courts. Its original jurisdiction extended to cases of disbarments or impeachments of lower court judges and to determining questions of law and fact that affected its appellate jurisdiction. Its appellate jurisdiction extended to all civil cases that involved a minimum of four thousand dollars and to criminal cases where death or life imprisonment were imposed. Unlike civil matters, it could only rule on questions of law. The courts of appeal could decide questions of fact that bore on its appellate jurisdiction. They took civil appeals from the district courts where the amounts were above one hundred dollars and less than four thousand dollars, as well as criminal cases other than those that went up to the Supreme Court. As for the district courts, they were the tribunal of first instance in any civil cases where the value was either unspecified or more than fifty dollars. They also exercised original jurisdiction over probates, successions, divorces, emancipations, adoptions, interdictions, tutorships, curatorships, receiverships, disputes about titles to real estate or public positions, suits about civil or political rights, and criminal cases.

Spencer withdrew the General Assembly's power to regulate pleading, practice, and procedure in the courts by statute. He transformed the existing laws into the operative rules and allotted the authority to change or add to them to a special council of judges. The council was prevented from making alterations only after there was notice, hearings, and the approval of three-fourths the members.

Each branch of the courts sat for a specified time. The Supreme Court met annually in New Orleans from October to June. To distribute the work more evenly and to move it along more expeditiously, Spencer divided the court into Section A and Section B. Section A consisted of the chief and three associates; Section B was composed of the chief and three different associates, and each section held rehearings or heard arguments on alternate weeks. The justices could sit in sections or en banc as it suited the business and convenience of the court. Any case that failed the approval of a section was decided en banc as did any case that failed to win four votes in the full Court. Once the justices came to their decision, the chief either wrote the opinion himself or he assigned it to an associate before he read it from the bench and the clerk entered it on the minutes. The courts of appeal convened according to a similar calendar and work schedule as the Supreme Court and the district courts sat monthly.

Spencer patterned the most eye-catching part of his plan on a model he borrowed from the AJS. It was a board with vast supervisory powers over the management and regulation of the courts.[x] Styled the Supreme Judicial Council, it was comprised of the chief justice, three associates, the chief judges of the court of appeal, and judges from the district courts. It convened semiannually or any time at the call of the chief justice or three members. The clerk of the Supreme Court acted as its secretary, and its records were available for the public's inspection. It could recommend changes in the number of district court judges to the General Assembly, and it could change or abolish any court's rules of pleading, practice, and procedure. The Supreme Judicial Council could manage the judges and judicial business, and if necessary, either it or the chief justice could assign a judge from one court to sit in another. Additionally, it named and supervised the district judicial councils that implemented these and its other mandates.[63] It appointed committees to investigate ex parte allegations of misbehavior or "conduct unbecoming" of lower court judges, and it was required to forward their reports to the house of representatives or the attorney general for impeachment or removal proceedings. At its discretion it could suspend an accused pending the outcome of the charges against him. The Council prescribed the standards for admission to the bar and lawyerly deportment, and it wrote the rules for adjudicating disbarment eases. Then there was provision for a select committee of attorneys that looked into any matters and things over which the Council held jurisdiction. Lastly, the General Assembly and the Council were authorized to confer from time to time about widening the ambit of the Council's powers.

Discussion of Spencer's report was as intense as the spread of opinions about it was broad. To certain critics it was premature, and they attacked Spencer for bringing it up. One critic said, "I don't know whether he is a railroad lawyer, or not, but if he is not, then he wants to railroad this with the rapidity of an electric current."[y] Some delegates were leery merely because of its novelty. Others were dubious because it borrowed from progressive ideas that they disdained. Several country speakers saw the plan as the latest evidence of the New Orleanians domination of the association. The members who also sat in the General Assembly liked the judiciary provisions but opposed Part A as

63 There were four of them. Their composition and responsibilities were set forth in art. XXX.

far too limiting on their authority. There were those, including Chief Justice Charles A. O'Niell, who thought Spencer's modernist views of the role of the chief justice and the Supreme Judicial Council were too radical departures for a system that needed only tinkering around the edges. Even some on the special committee had doubts, but Spencer's forceful arguments and President Edward T. Weeks's control of the discussion carried the day. Then too, everyone recognized whatever became of the plan was wholly dependent upon how it would fare in a soon-to-be called convention to abolish the much maligned Constitution of 1913. That call never came.

Spencer's plan was shelved but not forgotten. It came briefly off the shelf when reform-minded delegates tried to push the constitutional convention of 1921 toward a radical restructuring of the judiciary. They invited Spencer and O'Niell to address the convention about ways to fix the courts. Spencer pitched his scheme. The only part that O'Niell favored was raising the number of justices from five to seven, and his resistance effectively returned the Spencer plan to the shelf in the association's archives.[z]

Given his approach to being chief justice, O'Niell was more a jurist of the nineteenth century than of the twentieth. O'Niell worked at his own pace with little concern for schedules, rehearings, long delays, and clogged dockets. He was always skeptical of court reform as being little more than a lightly veiled attack upon him, although his skepticism was also consistent with how he saw himself as chief justice. That the chief justice was the top cop never sat well with him. Having no taste for the supervisory tasks that went with heading the third branch of state government, he was an indifferent administrator. He stood out as a relic of simpler times, which made him ripe for the charges of backwardness that dogged him, but members of the association, even his critics, treasured him, nonetheless.

The contrariety of views about O'Niell and the Spencer

plan were reflective of other tensions in the association that led to its restructuring in 1929. To certain members the association was unbalanced and unable to become what it set out to be. Its corporate offices and the library were in New Orleans. The *Annual Reports* were edited and published there too. Most presidents were Orleanians as were committee chairmen.

Members were classified first as Orleans members and second as country members, and a reminder of that classification always appeared in the *Annual Reports*. A New Orleanian called P. M. Milner spoke to the imbalance during a debate about the membership article in the charter at the annual meeting in 1915. To Milner, the association had become an association in name only because of its inability to direct who should be judges or to control legislation. It would continue to lack that vital "punch" until it recruited every eligible reputable attorney to wear their membership in "the Louisiana Bar Association [as] a badge of honesty and competency and of fidelity to trust."[aa] Those desirable would not join, he said, unless the association was "revolutionized" to attract more than the fifty to seventy-five delegates that attended annual meetings. His remedy was ending the distinction between the Crescent City and the country. Milner's words were as follows:

"By what prerogative is New Orleans to get all the honor and glory of this association? Why is the man from Orleans any more worthy of being a member of this association than any man from this whole state? Why should we make a dividing line between us of Orleans and you of the country? . . . I want to knock down that fence" (Milner).

Milner's "revolution" never happened, but in 1923 outgoing president Fred G. Hudson Jr. revisited the issues Milner had addressed nearly a decade before. Like Milner, Hudson pointed to the lack of membership as the problem, which he said had become a "bromide," but resolving it was still a key to "a strengthening of our standing and widening our influence."[bb] To Hudson, the association's activities and responsibilities were "too superficial," and it was "more poorly organized and less efficiently regulated than the humblest trade" (Presidential Address). Therefore he argued for structural changes to the presidency and the committees and for the General Assembly to invest in the association with more defined statutory powers. Among the latter, he argued, should be the right to maintain professional standards; tighter means of disciplining miscreant attorneys; greater say in legal education and bar admissions;, and the imposition of its code of ethics statewide. Nothing came of Hudson's efforts.

An abysmal postwar economy exacerbated social unrest and impoverished an already debt-ridden populace, but the association did next to nothing to dissipate the rising discontent. In fact, it always held the lower classes in such contempt that it never used its influence to ameliorate their plight. It was quiet in the prewar years when lynching was on the rise and the Ku Klux Klan was on the loose. Such influence as it had with the General Assembly was employed in guarding the interests of corporate clients or furthering its position in the legal fraternity. Help from the state government was opposed, because it would encourage laziness and unwillingness to seek private employers. Given the short end of a thin stick, down-and-out voters flocked to Huey P. Long, known as the Kingfish, as their savior. To them, Long was everything members of the association were not.

A largely self-taught attorney from Winnfield, Louisiana, Long's knowledge of the law and what could be made of it surpassed those who sported gilt-edged legal credentials. Smart, devious, and cunning he was a master manipulator who thirsted for absolute power. Traditions and nice manners meant nothing. Although he could be unbelievably crude, he had the unfailing gift of making his followers believe he was one of them. He was a mesmerizing stump orator and equally adept at using radio to extend his searing, sometimes humorous diatribes across the state. When he first appeared on the political scene, the respectable members of the LBA dismissed him as a boorish clod until he was elected governor. The day before his inauguration, Long was invited to talk to the 1928 annual meeting on a topic of his choosing in the apparent expectation that he would speak about the ways he would cooperate with the association. Long attacked the courts, judges, and members as corrupt tools of big corporations and decidedly out of step with the needs of the people whose paladin he was, and he vowed to ram changes through the General Assembly.[cc]

The speech startled Long's audience into the realization that the governor-to-be was an imminent threat. Meeting the threat demanded action, action meant mobilization, and mobilization meant recruiting every "good lawyer" to the association's standard. The immediate step was to revamp the organization and fashion the charter into a recruiting tool. A select committee transformed the existing charter into an instrument that spoke to a modern bar and political realities, and it was enacted at the 1929 meeting at Lafayette.[dd]

There were similarities between the new charter and the old one. Both were alike in length, approximately six printed pages. The number of articles remained the same, they embraced the same subjects, but the content was decidedly different. Instead of proposing amendments to the existing charter, the committee changed everything. They incorporated parts of old articles into new ones, and the badly outdated parts were either purged or modernized. The first article abolished its predecessor. In its stead was a one-sentence statement saying that henceforth the name of the organization was the Louisiana State Bar Association, and it was domiciled for ninety-nine years in the City of New Orleans. There was a much slimmer version of the old Article II. It succinctly declared the objects of the association to be "advance[ing] the science of jurisprudence, promot[ing] the administration of justice, uphold[ing] the honor of the profession of the law and encourage[ing] cordial intercourse among its members; to maintain[ing] a library in the City of New Orleans . . . and, generally, to promot[ing] the welfare of the profession in the State."[ee] Article III broke significantly with the past. It scrapped Henry Plauché Dart's code of ethics and replaced it with the American Bar Association's current, infinitely more comprehensive canon.[64]

The existing language in Article IV relating to the Executive Committee vacated presidential duties that were deemed unnecessary. Article V kept all of the standing and select committees that were created after 1910. It also provided a new standing committee on professional ethics that was to interpret the new canon of ethics and to explain "proper professional conduct" (Art. V) for members. It was also supposed to cooperate with the ABA and local associations to elevate "the ethical standards of the profession" throughout Louisiana (Art. V).

A revised Article VI defined membership anew. It reduced the categories to members and members ex officio. Any licensed attorney "in good standing" and full-time professors at the state's law schools might be inducted into the association. Members ex officio were state and federal judges who were granted all of the rights of membership but they could not vote. It eliminated an old charter amendment from 1914 that declared "the association, being non-political in character, shall not endorse any candidate for judicial office; but shall have and exercise the right to condemn any unworthy person who offers." Back then it was possible for the association to pretend to be "non-political," which it never was but now saying it was "non-political" was an impediment.

Article VII was a refined iteration of the association's role in investigating and disciplining miscreant attorneys. It also mandated that complaints against judges be referred to the Executive Committee "for such action as it may deem proper." Article VIII, containing information about meetings and dates, was unchanged. The ninth article altered the way the charter

64 The code of ethics was Article II in the order of the original charter.

could be amended. Under the old charter, the president proposed amendments and the Executive Committee approved them. They were seldom rejected because the committee who answered to the president were reluctant to oppose him. Now the charter could only be changed by a two-thirds vote of members at an annual meeting. And no amendment could come to the floor unless the secretary received a copy at least thirty days before a meeting and he sent copies to every member no later than fifteen days before that meeting.

Although the charter was adopted without dissent, it was not the favorite of all members. A minority of some size resented the speed with which it was done or they feared going up against Long, and a number resigned. Charles Fletchinger tried to keep everyone under the tent. In his presidential address to the 1930 convention he called attention to the attorneys' affirmative duty to participate in selecting judges and they should not refrain from it. The new charter allowed such participation but lacked the means of implementation so he promised to name a committee to devise one, which he did. It made no recommendations in 1931 apparently, because the meeting turned on lengthy, acrimonious debates about the judiciary and statutory revisals. A year later there was a five-page report that was debated for hours before the leadership whipped its adoption. So far as the records reveal, the association did not actively campaign in the 1932 primaries, so there was no confrontation with the Kingfish.

A skirmish was joined in a roundabout way, however. Allegations of fraudulent balloting in New Orleans during the 1932 election led Orleans Parish district attorney Eugene B. Stanley to launch an inquiry into the charges. Stanley had barely begun his investigation when Attorney General Gaston L. Porterie entered the case, which effectively put it on hold. Opponents of the Long regime immediately smelled rotten crawfish, believing that Porterie had intervened because there was something to hide and, more importantly, that Senator

Long was calling the shots. There was clamor for Stanley's probe to continue, but acting on Long's orders, Porterie declined to stand aside. His refusal cost him his membership in the LSBA.

President Joseph D. Barksdale narrated the sequence of events that resulted in Porterie's expulsion, and what the Executive Board considered unethical behavior. During the recent General Assembly, "the spoilsman [Senator Long] who held the power of patronage and public plunder in Louisiana" had come down from Washington, D.C. to attend the session.[ff] He cowed the majority into adopting "five pounds" of legislation that created new taxes, a new tax commission, and new bond amendments to the constitution and killing the minority's every effort to investigate what had become of already "exorbitant taxes" (La. Act. CXLI-CLI). The voters passed all of the constitutional amendments by substantial margins, but the returns from several Orleans precincts seemed suspicious. Consistently tiny tabulations indicated that the commissioners of elections in those precincts may have perpetrated voter fraud. Within weeks of the election, the press reported that the suspicions caused district attorney Eugene B. Stanley to empanel a grand jury to indict the commissioners if it found violations of the state election laws, but nothing in any of this interested the association as an association until Porterie intervened. Without warning he superseded Stanley and stopped the grand jury. Asked to explain himself, the attorney general wrote Stanley that any court action on his part would have deleterious effects on bond sales called for in the amendments. Porterie's intervention got the association's attention because Stanley had done nothing wrong and had acted true to his oath of office whereas Porterie's interference appeared to content Senator Long and the bankers who would profit from the bond sales.

An outraged Barksdale swung into action but was careful not to disrespect "the high office of Attorney General, the head of the Department of Justice in Louisiana under the Constitution." He secured the assistance of the New Orleans

Bar Association (NOBA), and on December 3, 1932, he publicly announced the formation of a six-man committee to look into the accuracy of the newspaper stories and the circumstances under which Porterie had acted. Three weeks later, the committee reported that Porterie had misapprehended any effects of the grand jury's investigation and had ignored their invitation to explain his position. They asserted both associations could no longer stay silent "while the liberties of the people are threatened, whether by force or by fraud in any election." Consequently, they counseled the Executive Committee to rescind Stanley's removal and direct him to continue investigating. If he would not then the executive committees of both associations must request the grand jury to proceed on its own initiative. A copy of the joint committees report and a letter went to Baton Rouge on December 29, 1932. It averred that neither association had fostered any attacks on the adoption of any constitutional amendments or the validity of any bond issue; their issue was upholding the law and its supremacy. Two days later Porterie's answer rehearsed his previous letters in part, and he wrote the matter was closed. The Executive Committee sent a letter to the grand jurors urging them to proceed on their own initiative; Stanley dissuaded them because no statutes sanctioned such a maneuver.

After Christmas, Barksdale put out another press release that explained the association's entry into the hubbub. It stood for law enforcement, and deplored the attorney general's action, which seemed a pretext for protecting constitutional amendments or the marketing of certain bond issues. Its belief in Stanley and the grand jury rested on two principles of paramount importance to the voters: guaranteeing the free expression of the popular will through the sanctity of the ballot box and guarding the chief bulwark of the liberty of the people, the grand jury, from any intrusion whatever on the performance of its duty. Shortly thereafter, charges of unprofessional conduct were lodged against Porterie.

Per Article VII of the charter, Barksdale referred the complaints to the standing committee on grievances which had the power to decide how Porterie should be punished, if at all. Hearing him out through his lawyer, the committee expelled the attorney general for "unprofessional conduct" and struck him from the membership rolls. Porterie appealed twice to the Executive Committee for rehearings but failed to follow through. In mid-June 1933, he attempted to resign, writing that he would have nothing further to do with more appeals or anything to do with such a political set-up, he heaped on the Executive Committee a generous verbal dollop of what Barksdale called the usual "crawfish" slime.[65]

Barksdale ended his narrative with the hope that this was the last and only time that the association would ever have to expel a high executive official time of the State of Louisiana. "The people," said he, "may look after his case when it comes to his reelection, but the bar association does need not wait until election time to voice its disapproval of such conduct." Certainly, a man who openly fiddled with a grand jury and substituted his opinion for the law of election frauds had "no place in this association. I do not care at whose behest he acted, but it is no excuse, to this association, that he acted at the behest of New Orleans bankers." On the other hand, he hoped that the association would never be so obsequious that it would sit silently and inactively whenever unlawful future attacks were made "on the very vitals of our State Government." The test of that hope would come in the judicial elections of 1934.

65 The members were John D. Miller, Henry McCall, Warren Doyle, Herbert W. Kaiser, William J. Guste, and Rene A. Viosca.

NOTES

a. Edward F. Haas, *Political Leadership in a Southern City: New Orleans in the Progressive Era* (Ruston, 1988); $_{WB}$Bennett H. Wall, et al., *Louisiana: A History*, 4th ed. (Wheeling, 2002), 243-308; Matthew J. Schott, "Huey Long: Progressive Backlash?" *Louisiana History: The Journal of the Louisiana Historical Association*, 27 (1986): 133-45; Samuel C. Shepherd Jr., "In Pursuit of Louisiana Progressives," *Louisiana History*, 46 (2005): 389-406; $_{WB}$Charles McGovern, *Sold American: Consumption and Citizenship, 1890–1945.*

b. "An Act to provide for the construction and maintenance of a court-house building in New Orleans . . .," La. act. LXXIX in Acts of La. (1902): 106-10, HeinOnline.

c. Courthouse Commission, "Minute Book," Louisiana Digital Library (October 17, 1902): 1-2.

d. "An Act to provide for the acquisition for, and or the construction and maintenance of a courthouse building in the City of New Orleans . . .," La. 96 in Acts of La. (1904): 214-21, HienOnline; "An Act to amend Sections 6 and 10 of Act No. 96 of 1904 . . .," La. act. CLXXIX in Acts of La. (1904): 369-70, HeinOnline.

e. Bernard McCloskey, "The New Orleans Court House," in *Annual Report of the Louisiana Bar Association, 1909* (New Orleans, 1909), 158-170: HeinOnline; Court House Commission, "Minute Book," (April 2, 1906): 154.

f. Courthouse Commission "Minute Book," (April 3, 1906): 158; "Contract with A. B. Stanard," Louisiana Digital Library: (March 1, 1907); Tara Lombardi, "Designing a Courthouse: The Winning Architects." *De Novo*, 8 (2010): 3.

g. Dart, "Address at the Corner-Stone Ceremonies" (New Orleans, 1908): Louisiana Digital Library; *The Times-Democrat* (New Orleans, La.), January 9, 1908.

h. La. Ann. 1929: HeinOnline.

i. Amendment to Article V of the charter, 1909.

j. Amendment to Article V of the charter, 1910.

k. "Our Judges: The Supreme Court of Louisiana," *The Times Picayune* (New Orleans, La.), May 1, 1887: 10; "Obituary" in *Annual Report, 1912-13*: 399; Glen R. Conrad, "Charles Erasmus Fenner," *Dictionary of Louisiana Biography Online*: Louisiana Historical Association.

l. "An act to promote the comfort of passengers on railway trains...and to repeal all laws and parts of law contrary to or inconsistent within the provision of this act," La. act. X in acts of La. (1890): 152-54, HeinOnline.

m. "Biographical Sketch," in La. Ann. 1930: 194-195, HeinOnline.

n. *Report of the Commission to Revise the Civil Code of Louisiana to Jared Y. Sanders Governor of Louisiana* (Baton Rouge, 1910), 23; John H. Tucker, "Source Books of Louisiana Law," *Tulane Law Review*, 6, no. 2 (1931-1932):297-98; W.O. Hart et al., *Report of the Commission on Uniform State Laws in Louisiana for 1914* (Baton Rouge, 1914); William O. Hart, "Women's Rights in Louisiana," *Louisiana Historical Quarterly*, 4 (1921): 437-58.

o. William M. Deacon, comp., *Reference Biography of Louisiana Bench and Bar, 1922* (New Orleans, 1922), 83; Henry E. Chambers, *A History of Louisiana, Wilderness–Colony–Province–Territory–State–People* (Chicago and New York, 1925), 3:297; "Obituary," *The Times-Picayune* (New Orleans, La.), June 22, 1934: 1,2.

p. Edwin T. Merrick, ed., *Revised Civil Code of the State of Louisiana* (New Orleans, 1900), Preface.

q. "Presidential Address," (May 6, 1905) in La. Ann. (1905): 3-6; "Presidential Address," (May 5, 1906) in La. Ann. (1906): 3-6.

r. "Obituaries," *The New Orleans Item*, March 16, 1941: 1,8; B Obituaries, *New Orleans Item*, 16 Mar. 1941:1, 8; *Morning Advocate* (Baton Rouge, La.), March 16, 1941: 1,6.

s. "Spencer's Resolution," in La. Ann. (1915): 75-76.

t. "Spencer's Resolution," 76-84.

u. "Committee Report, Final Draft of Articles Relative to Legislative Procedure," In Appendix A of La. Ann. (1916): 40-42.

v. "Committee Report, Tentative Draft of Articles Relative to Judiciary System," In Appendix B of La. Ann. (1916): 42-56.

w. "Article 8," in La. Ann. (1916): 45-46.

x. "Article 29," in La. Ann. (1916): 53-55.

y. La. Ann. (1916): 60.

z. *Official Journal of the Proceedings of the Constitutional Convention of the State of Louisiana Begun and Held in the City of Baton Rouge March 1, 1921*, HathiTrust (Baton Rouge, 1921): 35, 41.

aa. P.M. Milner, speech, (May 7, 1915) in La. Ann. 1915: 63-64, HienOnline.

bb. "Presidential Address" (May 7, 1915) in La. Ann. 1915: 200-2005, HienOnline.

cc. Huey P. Long, speech, (April 14, 1928) in La. Ann. 1928: 26, 77, HeinOnline.

dd. La. Ann. of the Louisiana state Bar Association (1929), 219-25, HeinOnline.

ee. Art. V.

ff. La. Act. CXLI-CLI in Acts of La. (1932): 501-506, HeinOnline.

Chapter Five

The Disputed Judicial Election of 1934

Nineteen thirty-four was a pivotal year for the Louisiana State Bar Association (LSBA). It turned in a direction no one anticipated, although it might have been foreseen, given the association's routine participation in electoral politics. The leaders of the LSBA were frustrated by their inability to combat what they viewed as the evils of Huey P. Long. To them, the general election of 1934 was their opportunity to put Chief Justice Charles A. O'Niell in control of the Supreme Court by defeating Winston Overton, a Longite justice who was up for reelection. They openly backed his opponent Thomas F. Porter Jr. The effort backfired. It provoked the wrath of Long and his minions who reduced O'Niell to a nullity and nearly destroyed the association.

* * *

Chief Justice O'Niell presided over the Supreme Court during what was undoubtedly the most tumultuous period in its history. O'Niell's undisguised contempt for Huey "the Kingfish" Long and all that he embodied, saturated the court with a partisanship never seen before or since. Long was no less disdainful of O'Niell. Their antagonism traced to Long's impeachment in 1929 and to O'Niell's role as presiding judge at the trial itself. Long's animosity deepened afterward, because O'Niell's jurisprudence stressed an independent judiciary and separation of powers as sturdy barriers against overbearing executive power, which were principles far distant from Long's way of government. Those differences were reflected in the background and attitudes of O'Niell's brother justices: Fred M. Odom, Wynne G. Rogers, Harney F. Brunot, John R. Land, John St. Paul, and Winston Overton. Odom and Rogers aligned with O'Niell, and they were popular with the LSBA. The others belonged to Long.

The chief justice (1869–1951) was born to an Irish father and an English mother who lived in the St. Mary Parish town of Franklin, Louisiana. He went to the town's public school and received a bachelor's of law degree from Christian Brothers College in Memphis, Tennessee. Attracted to the law, he apprenticed in the office of Governor Murphy J. Foster before he furthered his legal studies at Tulane University. Licensed to practice in 1893, he opened his office in Franklin. He was the first country attorney inducted into the LSBA and was one of its most active leaders until he became a district judge in St. Mary Parish. In 1912, he was elected an associate supreme court justice. A decade later. he succeeded Olivier O. Provosty as chief justice and held the center seat until he retired in 1949. Of a progressive bent, and inimical to the monopolies that controlled the Louisiana economy, he drifted toward reform minded politicians like Governor John M. Parker. As a jurist, O'Niell wrote eloquent, even witty opinions that were recognized nationally for their uncommonly fine draftsmanship. His weakness was his resolute resistance to modernizing the Supreme Court which opened him to charges of backwardness that dogged him for as long as he was chief. The flaw was a foil that the Longites repeatedly used to skewer him with near deadly effect.[a]

CHARLES A. O'NIELL from the Louisiana Supreme Court Portrait Collection, Law Library of Louisiana, New Orleans.

Born in Natchitoches, Odom (ca. 1871–1960) received an undergraduate education at Louisiana State Normal School (now Northwestern State University) before he went on to read law. He was elected Shreveport's district attorney in 1908. After holding that post for a decade, he ran for and won a district court judgeship. On the bench he gained renown as the judge who tried and convicted four members of the Morehouse Parish Ku Klux Klan, several of whom were his friends. Afterwards he fended off the Klan's attempt to defeat him when he stood for a seat on the Second Circuit Court of Appeal. He became a member of the Supreme Court in 1930, where he stayed until his retirement sixteen years later. As a justice he was at odds with Long whom he grew to loathe, which drew him to O'Niell.[b]

Wynne G. Rogers (1874–1946) was a member of the New Orleans legal and social establishment through and through. His father was a lower court judge and an uncle had been an attorney general of Louisiana. He was locally educated and graduated from the Tulane Law School in 1895. Admitted to the bar in 1896, he affiliated with his uncle's firm prior to his partnering with Bernard Titche. He was active in the Louisiana Bar Association (LBA), which he joined right after he became an attorney. In 1920 he accepted a chair in civil law at Tulane. He held it for half a decade until, like his father and his uncle, he felt the pull of the bench, and he took a seat on the Orleans civil district court. The retirement of Justice Joshua G. Baker in 1922 created a vacancy on the Supreme Court, and Rogers was elected to fill it. Two years later he ran unopposed for a full term. He was reelected in 1938 and died in office. Everything about Rogers put him at odds with Long, and he typified Louisianans who detested Long as much for who he was as for his hand on the tiller of state.[c]

Justice St. Paul (1867–1939) sat on the Supreme Court for twelve years. Born in Mobile, Alabama, he was the son of Amanda Pocheu St. Paul de Lechard and Henry St. Paul de Lechard, an attorney and former Confederate army officer. He received his law degree from Tulane when he was twenty-one, he went into private practice, and he joined the LBA . While serving a single term in the state senate, St. Paul helped draft the Constitution of 1898. Governor Murphy J. Foster named him a civil district court judge before Governor Jared Y. Sanders elevated him to the Court of Appeal. He went to the Supreme Court in 1922. In addition to his judicial activities, St. Paul was the founding dean of the law school at Loyola University of New Orleans, and he was chiefly responsible for recruiting its first faculty, which included his colleague Joseph A. Breaux and some prominent New Orleans attorneys.[d]

Given that background, it is safe to say that St. Paul had little love for Long. If anything, he should have lined up with O'Niell, Odom, and Rogers, but he did not. Instead, he sustained Long's legislative programs whenever they came up for adjudication by the Supreme Court. The explanation seems to have been personal and philosophical. Personally, he upheld Long because his son was one of Long's operatives in New Orleans.

Philosophically, it was his view that the court should restrain the General Assembly only when it unmistakably strayed from its constitutional boundaries, and he seldom decided that it did. So, he sided with Brunot, Land, and Overton, thereby ensuring Long control of the Supreme Court, but barely.

John Land (1862–1941) was the third member of his family to sit on the Supreme Court. A native of Lexington, Mississippi, he went to school at Thatcher's Academy in Shreveport and Washington and Lee University before he was admitted to the bar in Shreveport. He was in private practice prior to his election to the state legislature in 1888. After one term in the house, he became district attorney for Caddo Parish, an office he occupied for twelve years. He moved on to a district court judgeship in 1912. A decade later, he was elected to a newly created seat on the Supreme Court. That he never belonged to the LSBA as a dues-paying member suggests his disdain for it as well as a reason for his being within the Long orbit.[e]

Harney F. Brunot (1860–1944) was from Catahoula Parish. He attended Christian Brothers College in Pass Christian, Mississippi, Cooper's Institute, and Louisiana State University (LSU) before he graduated Tulane Law School and was admitted to the bar. He became a city attorney for Baton Rouge and a district judge. On the bench, Brunot incurred Long's wrath when he convicted Long for libeling Governor John Parker and hampering a lawsuit against the Standard Oil Company. When he stood for the Supreme Court, he ran on an anti-Ku Klux Klan ticket and staved off the Klan's attempt to defeat him. Long never trusted Brunot even after he swore allegiance to him but by becoming a Kingfish man, Brunot kept his seat for over two decades before he retired.[f]

Justice Overton (1870–1934) rose to manhood in Marksville, Louisiana.

WINSTON S. OVERTON from the Louisiana Supreme Court Portrait Collection, Law Library of Louisiana, New Orleans.

His father and grandfather had been local district court judges, and his great-grandfather, General Thomas Overton, had been a longtime friend of Andrew Jackson. His older brother John was a United States senator and a pliant Long ally. After Justice Overton graduated Louisiana State University, he read law with his father and took law courses at Tulane before he qualified as an attorney in 1892. Thereafter he was city attorney for Lake Charles, a district court judge, a delegate at the Constitutional Convention of 1921, and chairman of its judiciary commission before he went to the Supreme Court. Lawyers and laymen alike regarded him as a first-class jurist who was "able, honest, dedicated, conscientious, competent," and unusually well-versed in the law.[g] An attorney who knew of him remembered that no one ever said anything derogatory about him but went on to recall that he was so engrossed in his work that he was often absentmindedly forgetful of other things. Overton's family supported the Kingfish and brother John. Overton followed suit, though he was not outspoken, but his rulings upheld Long. The voters in his supreme court district knew where he stood, and it made little difference to many of them, even those who were not fond of Long (Deacon, 44).

In the spring of 1934, Long was bent on keeping the Supreme Court in his pocket. The likelihood of his doing so seemed safe as the primary season neared. Only Overton was up for re-election. Overton was sure to draw an opponent, but Long appeared confident of his prospects. He was the incumbent, and that was greatly to his advantage. Odds were he should handily win in the primary which meant he would hold the seat and Long would keep his majority. But an unanticipated hitch complicated those calculations. Citing declining health, Justice St. Paul announced in April that he would retire when Court adjourned for the summer recess.[h] Long's lackey governor Oscar K. Allen[66] could not appoint a successor, however, because twelve years remained on St. Paul's term. According to the Constitution of 1921, a vacancy of that length could only be filled by a special election "called by the Governor, which shall be held within four months after the vacancy shall have occurred."[i]

Open seats always threatened unpredictable results, and in this instance the outcome was even more volatile. St. Paul represented the First Supreme Court District, comprised of Orleans, Jefferson, St. Bernard, St. Charles, St. John, and Plaquemines parishes. Orleans Parish was the citadel of Long's bitter enemy Crescent City Mayor T. Semmes Walmsley.[67] Seizing the opportunity to break the Kingfish's control of

66 Long picked the ever-loyal Allen (1880–1936) to succeed him as governor. See William D. Pedersen "Oscar Kelly Allen," *Dictionary of Louisiana Online*.

67 T. Semmes Walmsley (1889–1942) led a faction of Louisiana Democrats that opposed Long. He served as mayor of New Orleans from 1930 to 1936. See Michael L. Kurtz, "T. Semmes Walmsley," *Dictionary of Louisiana Biography Online.*

the Supreme Court, Walmsley backed a New Orleans district judge, Walter Gleason, who also drew the immediate vigorous endorsement of the LSBA.

To counter Walmsley, Senator Long tapped Algiers, Louisiana, native Archibald T. Higgins to oppose Gleason. Called "Archie" by everyone, Higgins (1893–1945) was a sharp-minded, appealing, well-liked appellate court judge. He was born across the Mississippi River in Algiers but grew up in nearby Gretna. After high school he earned a Bachelor of Laws from Tulane and a Master of Laws diploma from Loyola University. He was an associate in former Governor Luther E. Hall's law firm until he left to practice on his own. His real interest was in politics, and he was successively city attorney for Gretna, an assistant district attorney in Jefferson Parish, a state representative, and a district court judge. Then he was appointed and later reelected to a vacancy on the Fourth Circuit Court of Appeal. He cast his eye on bigger things when he learned of St. Paul's resignation, so he enthusiastically agreed to Long's offer.[j]

Certain that he had a winner, Long flung himself unabashedly into the Higgins-Gleason match. That commitment left Winston Overton to fend for himself. Even though Overton was the incumbent and could depend on Long's vocal support, he soon found himself locked into a stiff fight with an energetic adversary, Thomas F. Porter Jr.

THOMAS F. PORTER From the William L. McLeod, Jr. Papers, Collection no. 159, Archives and Special Collections Department, Frazar Memorial Library, McNeese State University.

Porter (1881–1963) was a native of Natchitoches Parish. Educated collegiately at nearby Louisiana State Normal School, he taught school in Calcasieu Parish until he decided to study law. He matriculated at Yale University where he received his law degree in 1906. Back in Louisiana, he moved to Lake Charles, joined the LBA, and partnered with a local attorney, Edwin F. Gayle. He married Gayle's sister, Mary, and settled into the existence of a small-town lawyer. After Congress declared war on Germany in 1917, he volunteered for military service and saw action in France as an artillery officer. Returning to Lake Charles, he picked up where he left off with Gayle. The routines of the practice and family life soon made him itchy for a judgeship, and in 1920, he won a seat on the Fourteenth Judicial District Court. An ardent speaker, he was an eloquent, dexterous debater on the stump. When the opportunity to challenge Overton came, he jumped at the chance. He reckoned his own favor with voters and a coalition of local attorneys, politicians, or anyone else who hated Long, he could take the seat away from Overton. Despite his reputation as a skilled, fair judge, he did not enjoy the affection that was shown to Justice Overton. Litigants who came into his court characterized him as a strict disciplinarian who was usually irritable, overzealous, opinionated, and occasionally abusive. While those qualities were not evident when Porter campaigned, word of mouth made them known to the voters.[k]

Despite their differences in personality and politics, Overton and Porter were not enemies. Lake Charles was home to both. Their residences and offices were nearby one another, and they knew each other as professional colleagues. Both were Episcopalians who attended the Church of the Good Shepherd and contributed to restoration of the building after it was massively damaged by a hurricane. In a word, nothing suggests an abiding personal animus between them. Nevertheless, their contest would become personal. The person in question was neither of them; it was Huey P. Long.

The way the campaign worked was this: Before it could begin, the executive committee for the Democratic Party in the third supreme court district had to formally prepare for the primary election. To that purpose, the committee gathered in Crowley, Louisiana on July 3, 1934. As soon as the chairman T. Arthur Edwards[68] called the members to order, he recognized J. Cleveland Frugé.[69] Frugé moved a resolution that announced September 11 as the date of the election and called for candidates to file for the seat. It contained an additional requirement that only "electors of the White race" could vote.[l] Frugé's resolution was unanimously adopted. The committee scattered to wait for the outcome. As

68 T. Arthur Edwards (d.1962) was a Lake Charles attorney, a member of the LSBA, and a former district attorney.

69 J. Cleveland Frugé (1900–1991) was a lawyer from Ville Platte, Louisiana. In 1934, he was on a trajectory that resulted in his holding a variety of judgeships. After his retirement, he produced three biographical directories of Louisiana judges. See Carl A. Brasseaux, "J. Cleveland Frugé," *Dictionary of Louisiana Biography Online.*

soon as the results were known, it would reconvene to confirm them to Secretary of State Edwin A. Conway who would officially promulgate the winner as the party nominee.[m]

With less than seven weeks between qualification and election, speed was of the essence. The sheer size of the third supreme court district guaranteed that rapid courting of votes would be an especially exhausting exercise even for experienced stump campaigners like Overton and Porter. It comprised a huge area in the southwestern section of the state that included the parishes of Acadia, Allen, Avoyelles, Beauregard, Calcasieu, Cameron, Evangeline, Grant, Jefferson Davis, Lafayette, and Rapides. At the time these were mostly rural parishes that were not easily traversed over atrocious roads by automobile. Even so, the motor car was the quickest means of crisscrossing the district and reaching far-flung constituents.[70]

Long became the focal of the stump speeches. The gist of Porter's speeches was his furious attack on Long as a power crazed despot who would stop at nothing to undo constitutional rule. Overton was guilty by association because he always upheld Long's acts. Therefore, a vote for Overton was a vote for dictatorship while a vote for Porter was a vote to return to constitutional government. As for Overton, he downplayed the excesses that Porter accused of Long committing. Nothing in what he said was a disavowal of his attachments to Long. Instead he wooed his audiences by reminding them of the good things that had come to them because of Long.

Porter and Overton surely grew hoarse from speaking at as many as four rallies a day. They slept, ate, and changed outfits whenever and wherever they could. Such a frenzied tempo wore them down, but it played hardest on Overton. He

70 The Louisiana Department of Transportation and Development maintains a digital collection of historical road maps. A map that dates from 1930 is a good illustration of the condition of the roads in the district. It is accessible on their website.

was sixty-four-years old, and his reluctance to reduce his judicial responsibilities significantly impaired his health. Every appearance in the district began and ended with a five-hundred-mile round trip from New Orleans. A few days before the primary, he was at home in New Orleans when he felt sick, but neither he nor anyone in his family thought his indisposition was any more than a momentary upset. It was. A cerebral hemorrhage struck him dead on September 9, 1934, barely thirty-six hours before the election. That evening the body left by train for Lake Charles and his funeral.[n]

Newspapers and radio speedily reported Overton's death around the state. When word came to Porter, he immediately turned a campaign rally in Lafayette into a memorial observance. By late afternoon of September 10, family, friends, Justices O'Niell and Odom, the lieutenant governor, and other dignitaries were in Lake Charles. They assembled in the Church of the Good Shepherd. The Reverend George F. Wharton met the funeral party at the church doorway. He intoned the opening prayers of the burial rite as the pallbearers—including Lieutenant Governor John B. Fournet, Sheriff Henry A. Reid, and Edwin F. Gayle—briskly bore the casket down the long center aisle and placed it on a stand that stood before the altar. When Mr. Wharton finished the service Overton went to his grave in Graceland Cemetery.[o]

Voting went off as scheduled on September 11, and after the votes were in and counted, Porter had won by a margin of 9633 to 4985. Although the turnout was low, he carried all eleven parishes, some by wide tallies. No one had voted in two Evangeline precincts, and there were approximately one hundred voters who had handed in blank ballots in two Lafayette precincts. How to interpret the votes Overton garnered is tricky. Then, as now, there was no determining how many voters knew he was dead and voted for him anyway or who among them learned of his death only after voting for him. The uncertainty, and the fact that Overton had died within thirty-six hours of the polling, caused his backers in the district to claim that Porter was an unqualified nominee.[71]

That was not the position of the LSBA nor other anti-Long lawyers who loudly and publicly demanded that Secretary of State Conway certify Porter forthwith. Nor was it shared by the nominal Longite, T. Arthur Edwards. Thinking that nothing might happen awry, he had cast an absentee ballot on September 8 and had driven to Beeville, Texas, for a visit with his brother. A phone caller told him that the justice was dead around noon on the tenth and he left Beeville for the long trip home.[72] It would be too late to cancel the primary and declare Porter the winner before he could get back to Lake Charles. Torrential rains slowed him, so he did not reach Lake Charles till midday on September 12. When the local press interviewed him about Overton and the Porter situation, he stated that he had been the district attorney when the justice was a district judge. Overton had been a close friend for many years, and he remarked how the state had just lost "an eminent jurist and a good citizen."[p] Regarding Porter, Edwards said unequivocally that the judge "will be declared the nominee, being the only legal candidate before the people, whether he got a majority of votes or not since the lamented death of Justice Overton is the same as if he had withdrawn or been disqualified, leaving the field to Judge Porter" (Williams, 733). He concluded the interview with an announcement that the executive committee would convene at Crowley on the fifteenth when it would certify Porter to Secretary of State Conway.

By law, Edwards could recall the executive committee whenever he chose, but why he was delayed for four days is unfathomable. Possibly his friendship with Long and his own vote for

71 An exhibit, labeled "B" in the Porter v. Conway case set forth the official count.

72 Beeville is located roughly midway between San Antonio and Corpus Christi.

Overton may have influenced him. That theory would be conclusive except for Edwards publicly declaring Porter the party's nominee. On the other hand, he may have believed that a short respite would calm passions and result in the acceptance that his understanding of the controlling statutes was correct. Whatever he reasoned his decision redounded to Porter's great disadvantage.

Long learned that Overton had died almost as soon as it happened. On September 10, he declared to reporters that Porter was offensive to him. (With typical crudeness, he had once said of him "if I owned a whorehouse, I wouldn't let him pimp for me."[q]) Until the primary was over, he merely ranted about "the people always being entitled to an election" and insinuated that he might have to intervene legislatively.[r] Getting Judge Higgins elected and smashing Mayor Walmsley were Long's foremost concerns. Walter Gleason lost, and with the outcome in Long's favor, he sought a way to deny Porter. On September 12, Long drove up to Baton Rouge to meet with his principal lieutenants, and together they concocted a double-pronged scheme that took advantage of the lucky break Edwards had accidently given him. He told his follower George A. Foster and several others of the third district executive committee to ask Attorney General Gaston L. Porterie[s] for his legal opinion about the legitimacy of Porter's election.[t]

The opinion rested on Porterie's reading of the Primary Election Law of 1922.[u] He ruled that Overton's death, coming only hours before the election, inevitably invalidated the votes cast two days earlier. Necessarily, it followed that there must be a new primary before the general election because the act manifestly forbade picking a candidate by any means other than a popular vote. Then he asked if there was a lawful way to nominate someone without an election. His answer went straight to the point of Foster's query. Had Overton died a week or more before the election, then Judge Porter would rightly have been nominated. That was impossible because Overton's death happened just two days before the voters went to the polls.

So Porterie averred: "that provision of the law is read entirely out insofar as this case is concerned, and you are left to the other provisions of the law."[v] Whenever there is "ample time as there is in this case the spirit and purpose of our law is always best served by giving the people the right to an election. I rule that you should do so in this case. No candidate can complain over allowing the voters to settle the issue—I doubt that one could be heard to complain if the question is simply submitted to the voters to settle. I would say as a general matter of Committee activity that it would be presumptive to substitute yourself for the people in the selection of the nominee of the Democratic Party which is tantamount to election" (Porter v. Conway case file).

Porterie ignored an operative section from a 1924 statue that amended the Primary Election Act . It plainly said, "That in the event that after the date has passed on which candidates are allowed to enter and file their notification in any primary, . . . one or more of the rival candidates . . . shall die, new candidates . . . shall be permitted to enter and file their notification for a period of five days after such death; *provided, that this provision shall not be effective when the death occurs within seven days of the date fixed for the primary election,*" (Italics added for emphasis).[w] Porterie's oversight was premeditated. It effectively gave legal cover to the more underhanded prong in Long's scheme, taking over the executive committee and holding a second primary that would elect a Kingfish man.

Long's scheme was no mystery. An article in the September 24 issue of the *Lake Charles American Press* reported rumors of the intention to overthrow Edwards and to seize control of the executive committee. It quoted T. Arthur Edwards as taking those rumors "calmly" and expecting "something like that."[x] But he said, "I am convinced it would not stand up in court. Reorganization of the committee wouldn't be legal; if reorganization had been intended, it should have been done when the committee met to call the primary election" (*The Lake Charles American Press*). As he ended the interview, he repeated his belief that Judge Porter had fairly and legally won the nomination.

On September 15, the executive committee went to the Crowley courthouse. Porter went too. So did Long and Lieutenant Governor Fournet, who was rumored to be Long's choice as Overton's replacement. By virtue of being a member of the Democratic state central committee, Porterie showed up as well. (Long intended his presence to reinforce his written opinion.) Outside, Long cornered Edwards and tried to convince him to back another primary. Edwards was unmoved. Hot words were exchanged, and as they separated, Edwards was overheard saying that he was no longer a follower of "'der furore' [sic] of Louisiana politics."[y]

Gaveling the meeting to order, Edwards called on C. F. Hardin who proposed Porter's certification.[z] Before there was a second, one of Long's men, J. W. Bolton, interjected that no business could proceed until a permanent chairman and secretary were elected. Edwards ruled Bolton out of order, but Bolton appealed to the committee. On a vote of eleven to four they overrode Edwards. Now Bolton proposed two more of Long's men, J. Cleveland Frugé and L. B. De Bellevue, for the offices, and the nominations carried, again by a division of eleven to four. Frugé took the chair and recognized Porterie, who recapped his ruling that by law the committee must arrange for another primary. When he finished talking, a resolution was passed that called for a new primary to be held on Tuesday, October 9.

According to a press report, Porter's temper bested him. He leapt onto a chair and screamed that he was the legitimate nominee and bawling that he would take his case to law. Now a restrained Kingfish could be quiet no longer. He jumped up and bellowed "All we want" is an election. The people are very jealous of an election. I'd hate to think I was claiming a nomination over the graveyard. I'd hate to think we had a graveyard candidate."[aa]

Then he stuck a finger in Porter's face and hollered "You're afraid to face the people."

After Porter called Long "a personal coward," Frugé calmed

them and adjourned the committee until noon on Friday, October 12, "for the purpose of canvassing the returns of [the] . . . primary and certifying the results, etc."[bb]

Porter was left with two choices, seek relief in the courts or requalify for another run. He decided his best chance lay in going to law. Because right and law patently belonged to him, he thought no fair-minded judge could feasibly find against him. U. A. Bell, P. G. Borron, Joseph W. Carroll, C. F. Hardin, Luther E. Hall, Charles Vernon Porter Jr., Arséne Pujo, Edward Rightor, and even T. Arthur Edwards, immediately teamed up to represent Porter. All of them belonged to the LSBA and Bell was its incumbent president. By September 20, they were prepared to go to trial. While the Porter team was drafting their briefs, the Supreme Court accidently damaged their client's prospects. On September 17, Archie Higgins was picked to finish the remaining three-and-a-half months of Overton's term.[cc] Naming Higgins satisfied a clause in the Constitution of 1921 that required the Supreme Court to fill short-term vacancies with someone from somewhere outside the third district, and Higgins obviously fit the requirement.[dd]

Nothing in the record testifies to why the Supreme Court chose Higgins, and the choice was published in the *Lake Charles American Press* as a straightforward news story.[ee] If O'Niell had wanted to, he could have thwarted the nomination because at the moment he, Odom, and Rogers could outvote Land and Brunot. That the anti-Longs did not pick a different judge may have been a political choice to mollify the Kingfish, which is possible, although there is no evidence that that calculus entered into their thinking. Another possibility is a better explanation. All five justices looked upon Higgins's interim appointment as a way of giving him high court experience before he took his own seat, and the court had resorted to such appointments in the past. Bringing him up would also help them to reduce their congested docket. Moreover, since the remainder of the Overton term was short, perhaps none of them expected that they would face any controversies in the coming months.

Four days later John Fournet sent J. Cleveland Frugé a letter saying he would run. The letter accompanied his written notice to the executive committee of his intention, which Frugé promptly filed and made him an official candidate.[ff73] Fournet was an unlikely aspirant to the state's highest court. Having recently turned thirty-nine, he was a relatively young man, but, as in the past, youth had never impeded other successful candidates. His qualifications were slim to none at all, though slight credentials had not hampered others before him. What mattered most were his ties to Long.

John B. Fournet from the Louisiana Supreme Court Portrait Collection, Law Library of Louisiana, New Orleans.

By his telling, Fournet (1895–1984) was born to an impoverished St. Martinville family. He went to ramshackle secondary schools with leaky roofs, broken windows, no heat, and worn-

73 Fournet to Frugé and Fournet's notice, both September 21, 1934, Porter v. Conway case file.

out textbooks. His teachers lent him their books. With their encouragement he got an education degree from Louisiana State Normal School and taught school in nearby parishes until he matriculated in the law school at LSU.

His stay was short because he joined the army after the United States declared war on Germany. Returning to LSU, he restarted his legal studies and graduated in 1920. By then he was living in Jennings, where he opened his law office. His clients were mostly little people who were often cash poor, so they paid him with eggs, livestock, or food, if at all. To supplement the little money the practice brought in, he continued teaching part time. The deprivations of his own upbringing and those of the people in the area around Jennings, goaded him into politics.

Running as a populist in 1928, Fournet went to the state house of representatives. His keen intelligence and feistiness combined with a political shrewdness and a patient resolve, drove his tenacious dedication to bettering the state for the people he represented while restraining the corporate excesses, and the privileges of the well-to-do.

Fournet was suspicious of the newly elected Governor Long, until he realized that Long's prescriptions for Louisiana matched many of his beliefs. Long saw Fournet as a possible ally and made him speaker of the house. After he blocked Long's impeachment, Fournet was put into the number two slot on the Oscar K. Allen gubernatorial ticket in 1932. His uncompromising devotion to the social benefits of Longism and his wish to crush judges he viewed as reactionaries made him a ready partner in Long's scheme to keep Tom Porter out of Overton's empty chair.[gg74]

74 Fournet had the unique distinction of being speaker of the house, chairman of the pardon board, senator, president of the senate, lieutenant governor, acting governor, justice, and chief justice. My colleague Raphael Cassimere, Jr., and I extensively interviewed Fournet at length in the 1970s. Whenever we sought his evaluation of Long, he always vehemently insisted that Long had bestowed benefits upon Louisianans that were greater than his flaws. He maintained that those shortcomings were highly exaggerated by Long's enemies. As for his ties to Long, he pointedly remarked on how growing up poor made him into a

On September 20, Porter's attorneys appeared in the district courts in Ville Platte and Baton Rouge. At Ville Platte, they petitioned Judge Benjamin H. Pavy to call off the October 9, primary averring that Porter's nomination was an undeniable factual reality. Because their client had won, he undoubtedly "had a vested right in [the] office."[hh] Therefore, to deny Porter the office was to infringe his constitutional rights as a citizen of Louisiana and the United States.

Judge Pavy, who was a harsh Long foe, agreed to hear the case. He set the twenty-seventh as the hearing date and ordered the executive committee, or their counsel, to show cause why he should not stop the primary (Petition of Thomas F. Porter Jr.). Porter's suit in Baton Rouge was filed with Judge W. Carruth Jones. In it, the attorneys' arguments were like those presented to Judge Pavy, but they also prayed for orders to forbid Secretary of State Conway from "printing or publishing on the official ballots to be used in the general election . . . the name or names of any person or persons other than" that of Thomas Porter.[ii] Judge Jones granted the request, but he allowed the state five days to answer why after further trial his temporary restraining order should not become permanent.

On September 25, Secretary Conway's counsel, Attorney General Porterie, came before Judge Jones. Arguing from his brief, Porterie opened by making three procedural caveats. Firstly, he claimed the executive committee, not the secretary of state, should have been sued. Secondly, the issue before the court was a political matter which meant that Judge Jones lacked jurisdiction since the regulating elections belonged "to the political department of the Government."[jj] To drive home this point he continued it was settled law "that the courts [sic] do not have jurisdiction in election matters unless the statutes particularly confer it [, and] it is a general rule of law that the injunctive process of the court will not issue against election officials to control them in the discharge of their duties in the conducting . . . an election

populist who looked to politics as the means to a better Louisiana. In part, this paragraph derives from my notes of those conversations.

even though the election or the manner of holding [it] might be null and void" (Brief of Attorney General Porterie). Thirdly, if the "courts [were] not clothed with authority to substitute their action for that of the people, then Porter could not sue Conway.

Next, Porterie attacked the heart of the petition at length, insisting that it had no merits in law or public policy. Reiterating his earlier opinion, he denied that Overton's death automatically qualified Porter. Had that been the intent of the primary act of 1922, then the statute would have said so unequivocally, but it did not. (Once more, he ignored the amending act of 1924.) He was equally dismissive of the assertion that Porter won the most votes on September 11, because by any rational definition there had been no election that day. He added a sarcastic aside that most of the district voters never wanted Judge Porter anyway. Moving on to the contention that the district executive committee had illegally called a second primary, he stated that Judge Jones must "apply the dominating principle of the law—let the people participate and select their candidate."[kk] As a matter of public policy, a judgment in Porter's favor would jeopardize the state's social and political order and engender discontent among the Democratic electorate. That being so, warned Porterie, "The primary election law permits the dominance of the white race in the political affairs of our State" Preventing a second primary would so arouse the voters that they would rise up in anger and "go to the general election and not only not support the supposed nominee but fight him openly" For such "strong social, political and philosophical reasons," concluded the attorney general, the judge must dismiss Porter's petition, and he sat down.

Judge Jones immediately ruled against the state and issued an injunction to forestall the second primary. He summarized his judgment this way. "It is argued that the people have a right to elect their candidates. Is it fair to make the man who made a campaign make it all over again with different candidates and different issues? I believe that the law contemplates that there shall be an end and when death intervenes it is the end of it. The law is clear to me. The election is over, and Judge Porter is entitled to the nomination."[ll] At that, Porterie filed a notice that he would seek a writ of certiorari from the Supreme Court.[mm]

Long blasted Judge Jones's decision, which he refused to accept, when he addressed a Fournet rally in Oakdale, Louisiana that evening. He told the crowd that he continued to believe the primary would go forward on October 9, but if by some nefarious means, "they" stopped it, he exhorted the audience to show up for the general election, and he swore that he would do "something" to defeat Porter. Then he reminded them that people like them and him opposed Porter, because "Porter is against the laws I have had passed and they want to put him on the supreme court bench so he can declare those laws unconstitutional."[nn]

Porterie, Joseph W. Carroll, and Luther E. Hall left Baton Rouge and drove separately to New Orleans in the early hours of September 26. When they got to the courthouse, Porterie presented his petition for the writ of certiorari, prohibition, and mandamus. Carroll and Hall handed in their memorandum in opposition.[75] The clerk distributed copies to the justices, and within hours the Supreme Court granted Porterie his writ.

Judge Jones was commanded to send up a trial transcript without delay, and he was ordered to stay his injunction until the justices concluded how and when to resolve the case. Both sides anticipated that outcome, given that the Supreme Court was the forum of last resort in similar disputes. Porter's lawyers thought that the justices would docket a hearing within several days, but to their absolute astonishment Justices Brunot, Land, and Higgins assigned the return date on the writ to November 26. Scheduling the hearing for that day killed whatever chance Porter had of prevailing because it fell three weeks after the general election.

Brunot, Land, and Higgins had acted quite legally but not fairly.

---

75 Copies of both documents are in the Porter v. Conway case file, and each is dated September, 26, 1934.

According to its then current rules, any justice could grant petitioners hearing, just as Brunot had done. Land and Higgins joined with Brunot to make a number sufficient to grant Porterie's writ. Besides, only the Supreme Court decided whether to grant writs of certiorari, and when they did, it was well within their power to docket a hearing date whenever they chose. O'Niell, Rogers, and Odom were powerless. They needed four votes to dismiss the writ or to alter the hearing date. Of the three, Rogers and Odom wrote muted dissents that focused on the Supreme Court's manifold injuries to Porter's rights.[oo] A fiery O'Niell dissented, writing that "on account of the law's delays, which sometimes amount to a denial of justice, the granting of the order staying further proceedings in this case will result in depriving Judge Porter of his nomination, and of the office to which he aspires, no matter how the court may eventually decide the case on its merits."[pp]

Justice Higgins countered with the reasons why Brunot, Land, and he had favored Porterie.

Archibald T. Higgins from the Louisiana Supreme Court Portrait Collection, Law Library of Louisiana, New Orleans.

He vouchsafed the attorney general's analysis and buttressed it with generous helpings of citations from case law. Higgins excused scheduling hearings until November 26, as a matter of time constraints and the public's interest. Therefore, he opined, "we have . . . accomplished our purpose of doing substantial justice to all parties concerned. Such is the purpose of equity."[qq]. What was legal was per se unfair, but fairness was not a consideration, Higgins's words to the contrary notwithstanding. A primary would be held on October 9, Fournet would win, and the Supreme Court would still belong to Long. Investing in Higgins had returned a quick reward.

Crestfallen but undeterred by the bad news out of New Orleans, Tom Porter was not about to go away. He immediately signed up as a candidate and stopped his suit against the executive committee in Ville Platte.[rr] His campaign was never much of a contest. He faced the undivided might of the Long organization. Accompanied by bands and sound trucks, Long crisscrossed the district loudly admonishing the voters to vote for Fournet. As for Fournet, he relied on Long to do most of the talking. When he did speak, he was brief, and he offered vague pledges to do right by the people. Porter pressed on. The LSBA endorsed him and pulled out all the stops on his behalf. All over Louisiana, local bar associations, unaffiliated attorneys, some judges, and newspapers backed him too. But it was Judge Pavy who vindictively castigated the Supreme Court for its "trickery and corrupt devices" that took the fancy of the press statewide[ss]. Those devices allowed "three Long-controlled justices" to steal Porter's nomination (*The Times-Picayune*). The vehemence of his rebukes, and the attacks on Fournet by others, supercharged an already heated contest and raised the ire of the Long camp to ever greater heights. However, like Porter's own barbed speeches, they were no obstacle to Fournet. He won the primary by more than four thousand votes (*The Times-Picayune*).[76]

---

76 New Orleans *Times-Picayune*, Oct. 4, 1934. Both the *Times-Picayune* and the *Lake Charles American Press* covered the race extensively, and those accounts

After the poll, Long and his minions were in no mood for good will. They wanted revenge. Attorney General Porterie quickly petitioned the Supreme Court to dismiss Porter's suit saying that Fournet's election had rendered it moot.[tt] The justices agreed, and that was that.[uu] Porter was further humiliated in 1935 when his judgeship, along with Judge Pavy's, was gerrymandered out of existence. Always grousing that Long had broken the law and grabbed the seat on the Supreme Court that should have been his, Porter lived for another twenty years. After he died, his funeral services were held at the Church of the Good Shepherd, and he lies in Graceland Cemetery just a short distance from where Overton was interred.

Having neutered Porter, the Longites aimed at settling scores with the LSBA. Several sources had long fed Long's animosity toward the association. It was a state-chartered, private organization that had its corporate offices and library on the third floor in the publicly owned courthouse at 400 Royal Street. The library held one of the largest collections of lawbooks in Louisiana, but it was closed to nonmembers such as Long. Justices had been active members prior to being elevated to ex officio status. Ever since the 1840s, they nominated members to be bar examiners. More recently the Supreme Court appointed other members, when necessary, to recommend disciplinary action against accused malefactors anywhere in Louisiana's entire legal profession. Although the association was a statewide organization, it was ruled by conservative, socially prominent attorneys, which made it an object of the opprobrium

---

are the basis for this summary of the race. To his enemies, Fournet was a legal nobody who had stolen his seat on the Court. He proved otherwise and grew into his judicial robes. A champion of reforming the Court, for thirty-five years, he was the engine that transformed it into a modern judicial institution. Those achievements are often overlooked but they rank him with, say, François-Xavier Martin or George Eustis. See $_{WB}$Warren M. Billings, *The Supreme Court of Louisiana: A Bicentennial Sketch* (New Orleans, 2011), 43-47.

of Long; less well-connected, small-town practitioners; and the poorly educated country barristers, none of whom could ever join. When Long addressed the LSBA in 1928, he chastised it as a bunch of elitists who were in the thrall of corporate interests and proposed that they should accept all qualified attorneys irrespective of background. Association leaders were ill disposed towards Long as far back as when he sat on the Railroad/ Public Service Commission. To them, and others of their ilk, he was a crude arriviste and a foul-mouthed potential dictator who posed the greatest threat to the rule of law and honest government in Louisiana history. And as recently as 1932, they stuck their finger in Long's eye when they drummed Attorney General Porterie out of the organization for his having prevented an investigation of voting irregularities in Orleans Parish. Small wonder, then, that Long and his people were eager to smash the association.

Directly, a chance to do that came just ten days after the primary, and it was handed to them by none other than the LSBA. There was a called meeting of the association to deal with a written complaint from Burt W. Henry, Esmond Phelps, J. Zach Spearing, Charles E. Dunbar Jr., Charles F. Fletchinger, Edwin T. Merrick, J. Blanc Monroe, and Monte M. Lemann that called for expelling Justices Land, Brunot, and Higgins as ex officio members.[77] The complainants alleged that the three justices deliberately set the return date on Porterie's writ until after the primary was over in order to harm Porter.

"Said action," they wrote, "constituted a violation of the defendants' oath of office, by which they had solemnly sworn to discharge and perform the duties of their office faithfully and impartially."[vv] Thus, "it is respectfully submitted that the defendants . . ., Members of this association, are unfit to remain members of this association and should be expelled,

77 Spearing and Fletchinger were past presidents of the association. Phelps and Dunbar were partners, so were Monroe and Lemann.

and that this association should take such other and further action as it may deem proper."

Their submission was extremely contentious, and it led a number of members to resign. Apart from those resignations, there was at least one doubter on the board who questioned the propriety of acting on the complaint since the Supreme Court had yet to rule on the merits of Porter's case. The objection was disregarded, and the board took the charge. President U. A. Bell was obligated by the LSBA charter to assign the allegations to a select committee for an investigation and a recommendation.[ww]

Under different circumstances, Bell would have chaired the committee, but he stood aside since he was one of Porter's attorneys. Instead, Senior Vice President John D. Miller, named himself, Secretary-Treasurer W. W. Young, and two other members as chairs to the committee. Their investigation dragged into June 1935 when they reported that "The Justices have not seen fit to acknowledge our jurisdiction to the extent of answering the charges, although one of them [Higgins] requested an extension of the original period allowed for answering. Under these circumstances we direct that the complaint be dismissed without prejudice."[xx] But they extolled Burt Henry and the other complainants for their "high sense of duty" and "commendable courage" (Bar Association, 380-434).

Their recommendation was totally useless because in June 1935 the LSBA was struggling to survive. Indeed, it no longer existed as the state's premier bar organization that was closely tied to the Supreme Court. The attempt to expel Brunot, Higgins, and Land had given the Long forces a heavy weapon to blast the association where it would do the greatest damage, and they did not tarry before using it. At Long's command, Governor Allen summoned the General Assembly into a short special session a mere six days after the general election. Circulated on November 11, his call contained nearly fifty bills that Long expected the legislators to adopt posthaste. Among them, was a bill "To enact legislation to create a public corporation to be known as 'the

State Bar of Louisiana."[yy][78] Backed up by Long who constantly roamed both chambers, Speaker of the House Allen J. Ellender, and Senate President Lieutenant Governor Fournet whipped members into line and allowed no delays. Long's floor leader in the house, New Orleanian Edmund G. Burke, introduced the bar bill which went to the committee on ways and means. It cleared the committee in half an hour, it was adopted on a floor vote, and it passed through the senate with equal celerity. Governor Allen initialed the bill into law on November 21.

A six-page law defined the State Bar of Louisiana (SBL).[zz] Sections eleven and twelve established how it was to be set up. Governor Allen would nominate to the senate eight licensed attorneys as the initial board of governors. The eight would constitute a commission "to place this Act in operation and to organize the State Bar . . . and generally give effect to this Act."[aaa] They would also hold office until the people elected a new board in the 1936 congressional primaries.

Henceforth, anyone who was licensed on or before the statute came into force was automatically enrolled, and thereafter anyone who did not enroll was forbidden to practice. There were only two classes of members, active and inactive. Active members paid annual dues of three dollars ; the dues of inactive members was two dollars. Only active members could serve on committees, vote in meetings, and they were entitled to hold office (La. § 2-7, 34-38, 31,9-10, 19-30).

As Long intended, the SBL was a state agency subject to executive and legislative oversight, and it could be "changed or terminated at any time by an Act of the Legislature of the State of Louisiana."[bbb] Its offices were in Baton Rouge and New Orleans, although it could convene anywhere it wished. The corporate structure resembled that of the LSBA, but only just.

78 The New Orleans *Times-Picayune* published Allen's call on Nov. 12, 1. It gave daily coverage to the session until it adjourned. I fashioned this discussion from those reports and from the official journals of the house and senate.

It had a president, three vice presidents, a secretary, and a treasurer who performed the customary executive and fiscal duties. Incumbents served one-year terms, and there was no prohibition against their re-election. All the officers, chairmen, and committee members were hand-picked by a board of governors. The board enjoyed broad, exclusive powers that most prominently included setting standards of professional behavior, adjudicating complaints of attorney misconduct, fixing standards of legal education, and requiring applicants to pass an examination that the board designed and administered. Candidates need not have a law degree or a bachelor's diploma, though they did have to show they had read with a qualified lawyer for at least three years (La. § 21, 29-30).

The method of selecting governors was profoundly different from the way the LSBA chose their directors. Governors served for two years. Deemed public officials, they were subject to popular election. They represented each of the state's eight congressional districts from which they were drawn, and their terms coincided with those of members of Congress. Qualified voters were permitted to run in the primaries. If a candidate was an attorney he had to include in his filing papers an affidavit that disclosed the fees he received from private corporations that he had represented during the previous five years. Whenever a vacancy happened, it was filled by the state's chief executive with the advice and consent of the state senate.[ccc]

The statute had been enacted in such haste that three of its sections needed to be amended when Long forced Governor Allen to call the General Assembly back to Baton Rouge in December. He had meant for the attorney general to be an ex officio member of the board of governors. That proviso had been left out so it was written into the revised version of Section eight. In turn, its inclusion caused the amendments to sections eleven and twelve that incorporated the change.[ddd] Section forty-two delivered the coup de grace to the LSBA. Without naming the association, it drily stated "That all laws and parts of laws, grants and charters, contrary to or in conflict herewith be and the same are hereby repealed and rescinded."[eee]

To be sure, its architects could claim, as they did, that the act brought every lawyer into a single professional society, which was a good thing. They also suggested that the act shared a close kinship to the model bar law which the American Judicature Society (AJS) had advocated for decades. In fact, one of the author's, Long's sometime law partner Hugh M. Wilkinson, told his audience at the first SBL meeting that the act was primarily a copy of a California statute. In his presidential address to the same listeners, Attorney General Porterie was praised for preventing any danger of "the profession . . . being controlled by the sentiment of one part of our State as against another part of the State."[fff]

Veiling the amended State Bar Act of 1934 with benign pronouncements barely disguised what the Longites had done. Determined to corral O'Niell, Odom, and Rogers, they not only shot down the LSBA, they violated the Supreme Court. They untied a link between the Supreme Court and the LSBA that had existed for almost a century just as they undid the court's supervision of the bar that had been embedded in every state constitution since 1813.They stacked the leadership of the profession in favor of their cronies. They did away with a code of ethics. They placed no limitations on traveling or office expenses, they did not prevent officers from being paid, nor did they mandate annual outside financial audits. Their relaxed criteria for legal training and bar examinations cheapened rather than enhanced the quality of lawyering. Because illiterate laymen might well be elected to the board of governors, the composition of the board itself was fraught. And they entrained the dispersal of the LSBA's law library.

Clearly, the statute slaked Long's cravings for revenge as it played to his populist instincts and those of his followers. Whether the legal profession in Louisiana would become better for it was an open question. So was the fate of the LSBA.

Like a moth to a candle's flame, the LSBA had flown too close to Huey Long. Unlike the moth it did not burn up. It was scorched. Recovering from the injury would test its resiliency as it confronted its reduced status.

NOTES

a. $_{WB}$Janice K. Shull, *The Chief Justices of Louisiana: Life Sketches* (New Orleans, 2007), 56-69.

b. "Obituary," *The Times-Picayune* (New Orleans, La.), August 26, 1960: 1; Alton Earl Ingram, "The Twentieth Century Ku Klux Klan in Morehouse Parish Louisiana" (master's thesis, Louisiana State University, 1961); "Alleged Klan Members Found Guilty," *Madera Mercury* (Madera, Ca.) November, 6, 1923; "The Klan in Morehouse," *The New York Times*, January 11, 1923: 20.

c. "Obituary," *The Times-Picayune* (New Orleans, La.), September 16, 1946: 1; Carl A. Brasseaux, "Wynne Gray Rogers," *Dictionary of Louisiana Biography Online*: Louisiana Historical Association.

d. "John St. Paul, 72, Former Justice Expires at Home," *The Times-Picayune* (New Orleans, La.), November 6, 1939.

e. "Veteran Justice of the High Tribunal Taken by Death," *The Times-Picayune* (New Orleans, La.), April 19, 1941: 1.

f. "Hardy [sic] F. Brunot Succumbs at 83," *The Times-Picayune* (New Orleans, La.), March 12, 1944: 1; Ingram, "The Twentieth Century Ku Klux Klan," 113; T. Harry Williams, *Huey Long* (New York, 1969), 145-51, 177-79.

g. William M. Deacon, *Reference Biography of Louisiana Bench & Bar, 1922* (New Orleans, 1922?), 44; Vance Plauché, "Short Sketch of the Fourteenth Judicial District Over Fifty Years Ago, 1920–1925," *Louisiana History: The Journal of the Louisiana Historical Association*, 18 (1977): 240; "Winston Overton, Justice of High Court, Dies," *The Times-Picayune* (New Orleans, La.), September 10, 1934: 1, 9.

h. "Justice St. Paul Retired Because Health Declined," *The Times-Picayune* (New Orleans, La.), May 1, 1934: 1-2.

i. La. CONST. of 1921, art. VII, §7, HeinOnline.

j. James D. Wilson, "Archibald Thomas Higgins," *Dictionary of Louisiana Biography Online*: Louisiana Historical Association.

k. Henry E. Chambers, *A History of Louisiana*, (Chicago and New York, 1923), 2: 293, HathiTrust; Plauché, "Short Sketch of the Fourteenth Judicial District," 240.

l. "Resolution of the Executive Committee," (July 3, 1934) in the Porter v. Conway case file (No. 33147) which is in the clerk's office at the Supreme Court in New Orleans.

m. "Affidavit of Thomas A. Edwards,"(September 19, 1934) in Porter v. Conway case file (No. 33147).

n. *The Times-Picayune* (New Orleans, La.), September 10, 1934: 1.

o. "Judge Overton Final Rites Held at Lake Charles," *The Times-Picayune* (New Orleans, La.), September 11, 1934: 1; "Justice Overton Dies Suddenly on Eve of Election," *State-Times Advocate* (Baton Rouge, La.), September 10, 1934: 1.

p. *The Lake Charles American Press*, September 12, 1934.

q. As quoted in T. Harry Williams, *Huey Long* (New York, 1969), 733.

r. *The Lake Charles American Press*, September 10, 1934.

s. Glenn R. Conrad, "Gaston Louis Porterie (1885–1953)," *Dictionary of Louisiana Biography Online*: Louisiana Historical Association.

t. *The Lake Charles American Press*, September 13, 1934.

u. "An Act to provide for calling, holding, conducting and regulating primary elections . . .," La. act. 97 in Acts of La. (1922): 178, 201, HeinOnline.

v. "Porterie's Opinion," in Porter v. Conway case file.

w. "An Act to amend Sections 16 and 30 of Act No. 97 of the Acts of the Legislature of the year 1922," La. act. 215 in Acts of La. (1924): 397, HeinOnline.

x. *The Lake Charles American Press*, September 14, 1934.

y. *The Lake Charles American Press*, September 15, 1924.

z. "Resolution certifying Porter," (September 15, 1934) in Porter v. Conway case file.

aa. *The Lake Charles American Press*, September 15, 1934; "Resolution Calling for a Primary Election," Porter v. Conway case file.

bb. Executive Committee "Minutes," (September 15, 1934) in Porter v. Conway case file.

cc. "Order appointing Higgins," (September 17, 1934) in "Minute Book" 44, (June 8, 1934-Jan. 12, 1937): 29, Clerk's Office.

dd. La. CONST. art. VII, §7. Higgins was duly sworn on September 18, 1934.

ee. *The Lake Charles American Press*, September 18, 1934.

ff. "Fournet to Frugé," (September 21, 1934) in Porter v. Conway case file; "Fournet's Notice," (September 21, 1934) in Porter v. Conway case file.

gg. Mrs. Robert Schoenfeld, "Jean (John) Baptiste Fournet," *Dictionary of Louisiana Biography Online*: Louisiana Historical Association; $_{WB}$Janice Shull, *The Chief Justices of Louisiana: Life Sketches*, (New Orleans, 2007), 61-63.

hh. "Petition of Thomas F. Porter Jr.," (September 20, 1934); "Order for the appearance of J. Cleveland Frugé et al," (September 20, 1934) in Porter v. Conway case file.

ii. "Petition of Thomas F. Porter Jr.," (September 20, 1934); "Order for the appearance of E.A. Conway," (September 20, 1934) in Porter v. Conway case file.

jj. "Brief of Attorney General Porterie," (September 25, 1934) in Porter v. Conway case file.

kk. "Brief of Attorney General Porterie," (September 25, 1934) in Porter v. Conway case file.

ll. "Judgment of Judge W. Carruth Jones," (September 24,1934), in Porter v. Conway case file.

mm. "Porterie's Notice," (September 24, 1934) in Porter v. Conway case file. See also *The Lake Charles American Press*, September 25, 1934 and New Orleans *The Times-Picayune* (New Orleans, La.), September 26, 1934.

nn. *The Times-Picayune* (New Orleans, La.), September 25, 1934.

oo. "Dissents of Odom and Rogers," in Porter v. Conway, 159, So. 159 (La. 1934):725, 725.

pp. O'Niell's Dissent," in in Porter v. Conway, 159, So. 159 (La. 1934): 726.

qq. O'Niell's Dissent," in in Porter v. Conway, 159, So. 159 (La. 1934): 740.

rr. Notice of Intention to Run," (September 26, 1934) in in Porter v. Conway case file; "Motion of L. L. Perrault," (September 28, 1934), in Porter v. Conway case file.

ss. The Times-Picayune (New Orleans, La.), October 4, 1934.

tt. "Porterie Petitions to the Court," in Porter v. Conway case file.

uu. Porter v. Conway, 159 So. 741 (La. 1 934)

vv. "Complaint of Burt W. Henry, Esmond Phelps, J. Zach Spearing, Charles F. Dunbar Jr., Charles F. Fletchinger, Edwin T. Merrick Jr., Blanc Monroe, and Monte M. Lemann," (October 19, 1934) in Executive

Committee Minute Book (June 2, 1934–June 1937): 377-79, Louisiana State Bar Association, New Orleans.

ww. La. Charter of 1899. art. VII: HathiTrust.

xx. Bar Association, "Minute Book," 380-434.

yy. The New Orleans *Times-Picayune* published Allen's call on Nov. 12, 1. It gave daily coverage to the session until it adjourned. I fashioned this discussion from those reports and from the official journals of the house and senate.

zz. "An Act to create a public corporation to be known as "The State Bar of Louisiana" . . .," La. act. X in Acts of La. (1934): 70-75, HeinOnline..

aaa. La. § 2-7, 34-38, 31,9-10, 19-30.

bbb. La. § 21, 29-30.

ccc. La. §13, 14.

ddd. "An Act to amend and re-enact Sections 8, 11 and 12 of Act N. 10 of the Second Extra Session of the Legislature of 1934," La. act. XXI in Acts of La. (1934): 135-37, HeinOnline.

eee. La. §42.

fff. "Speech to the State Bar of Louisiana," (January 31, 1935) in *Reports the State Bar of Louisiana for 1934-35*, 1 (Baton Rouge?, 1935):163-64, HeinOnline; "Porterie's President's Address," (January 31, 1935) in *Reports the State Bar of Louisiana for 1934-35*, 1 (Baton Rouge?, 1935):163-64, HeinOnline.

CHAPTER 6

THE BAR ASSOCIATION REDUX

Both the Louisiana State Bar Association (LSBA) and the State Bar of Louisiana (SBL) adapted to the reality imposed by the State Bar Act of 1934. Senator Long left organizing the state bar to his underlings. He had other crawfish to boil, namely consolidating his absolute power over every part of state government and contesting Franklin D. Roosevelt for the presidency. His assassination in September 1935 split his lieutenants who rivaled to succeed him and who were spectacularly corrupt. Their shenanigans made a mockery of the SBL which never had a chance to be an effective challenger to the LSBA. Contrary to Longite expectations, the LSBA refused to go away. The LSBA met and its leaders sought cooperation instead of confrontation, although they prevented the American Bar Association from recognizing their rival. Back channel discussions about a possible merger went nowhere until the scandals of 1939 and 1940 led to a reform administration that encouraged the reconstitution of the Louisiana State Bar Association into its modern form.[a]

* * *

The SBL was organized at about the same time the LSBA was kicked out of its premises on the third floor of the Royal Street courthouse. Louisiana Governor Oscar K. Allen filled the empty office positions and appointed a board of governors from a list of Long's designees, and Attorney General Gaston Porterie was tapped for the presidency.[79] After the Supreme Court amended its rules to accord with the State Bar Act of 1934, Porterie convened the first board meeting in New Orleans in January 1935.[b] The meeting was given over to setting a date for a forthcoming bar examination and other organizational matters before it adjourned until the first of March.[c] Some weeks afterwards, both the SBL and its enabling legislation were defended by Hugh Wilkinson at the invitation of members of the New Orleans bar. The main thrust of his talk was a defense of the integrated bar and a lengthy comparison of the similarities of the State Bar Act of 1934 and a California statute which he maintained was the model for the Louisiana law.[d] Staff completed the enrollment of attorneys and collected dues. The bar examination went off as scheduled, it was followed by another one in the summer, and plans were made for the initial annual meeting at the Heidelberg Hotel in Baton Rouge in November.[e]

Among the highlights were Porterie's presidential address and talks by Justice John Land, and Dean Frederick K. Beutel of the Loyola Law School. Porterie reviewed the debate over qualifications for bar admissions, Beutel argued the necessity of uplifting Louisiana's educational standards, and Land defended the reduction of his Court's supervision of the bar. As to fis-

79 Aside from Porterie and First Vice President Hugh Wilkinson the others were: Austin Fontenot, second vice president; George Wesley Smith, third vice president; George Thomas McSween, secretary; and the other four governors Sigur Martin, Jean Jacques, "Jack," Fournet, Warren Willingham Comish, and John Howard McSween. George Thomas McSween was a Long law partner, the attorney for the state's inheritance tax collector, and the husband of Chief Justice O'Niell's daughter, Kathleen. John Howard McSween was a lawyer and banker from Alexandria. Adrian Joseph Caillouet was a Houma lawyer. George Wesley Smith was an attorney and one-time mayor of Rayville, Louisiana. Sigur Martin was an attorney and one of Long's floor leaders in the state senate. A distant relative of Justice Fournet, Jack Fournet was the sitting lieutenant governor. Warren Comish was a Northshore lawyer and Long operative. He was elected to finish an unexpired district court judgeship in 1941.

cal matters, a statement of income and disbursement revealed that there were 1,855 attorneys whose enrollment had brought 5,400 dollars into the treasury. It also showed that all but 1,100 dollars was spent on supplies, the two bar examinations, travel, salaries, and miscellaneous expenses. None of the latter categories was itemized which conveniently hid who among the officers got what.[f] Before the conference ended, the board of governors announced their appointees to standing committees, but the identities of those individuals went unmentioned. Attendees scattered, not imagining that they had just been to the only annual conference the SBL would ever hold.

The disappearance of most of its archives precludes more than a cursory depiction of how the SBL functioned before its dissolution. In the merest of detail an extant minute book recorded the actions of the board of governors that were mainly concerned with admissions to the bar.[80]

All of the members of the Board of Governors of the SBL ran and were elected in the 1936 congressional elections but half of them were replaced two years later.[g81] The presidency passed from Porterie to Hugh Wilkinson. There were persistent rumors from the outset that the SBL Board of Governors consistently misused funds of the legal organization, but the allegations were neither proved nor disproved because the evidence was difficult to uncover. It should have been in the mandated reports that were never filed with

80 Now in the archives of the modern LSBA in New Orleans.

81 Edward Leland Richardson, who replaced George McSween, was an assistant attorney general who was general counsel for the Louisiana State Department of Revenue, a member of the Louisiana Revenue Commission, and vice chairman of the Interstate Oil Compact Commission. Edward D. Gianelloni, who replaced Adrian Caillouet, was from Napoleonville and the publisher of *The Assumption Pioneer*, which was the newspaper of record for the town and the parish. David M. Ellison was Governor Richard W. Leche's private secretary before he became attorney general and was implicated in the scandals of 1939 and 1940. Ellison took Austin Fontenot's place. K. K. Kennedy replaced George Wesley Smith.

the state treasurer. Complaints circulated about the board's neglect of defining bar admissions standards and preparing competent bar examinations. Equally problematic was the board's delays or outright unwillingness to investigate charges of attorney misconduct. Perhaps typical of that behavior was an incident which happened in March 1938. Independent of one another, two recent graduates of the Tulane Law School informed Dean Paul Brosman "of serious irregularities in the conduct of the bar examination held in Baton Rouge by the State Bar of Louisiana."[h] After consulting with his faculty the dean lodged a statement of charges with SBL President Hugh Wilkinson. Disbarment proceedings were subsequently filed in the Supreme Court against three attorneys who were charged with having conspired to give the four students the questions on the recent bar examination. The court immediately prevented the students from ever taking the examination again but the lawyers, including a member of the SBL Board of Governors went undisciplined.

Rampant and injurious though they were, corruption, malfeasance, graft, or other transgressions do not wholly explain the ultimate failure of the SBL. Those diseases were curable which made them more proximate than fundamentally constitutive. The root causes lay in the State Bar Act of 1934. Enacted in a moment of malice aforethought, it unbalanced the traditional legal order and drew immediate hostility from established attorneys who voiced what grew increasingly clear after 1935. The State Bar Act so hamstrung the SBL that it would never function properly.

Instead of striking the tent and retreating into extinction, the LSBA pressed on. In January 1935, the Executive Committee unanimously adopted W. Pike Hall Jr.'s, defiant resolution that "this association should be maintained and that its future course should be submitted to the entire membership at its annual meeting to be held at Alexandria, in the Spring of 1935."[i] The LSBA annual meeting assembled as scheduled in April, while the General Assembly sat and Huey P. Long was still in the state. It went off much as in the past. Officers were elected, standing committees were appointed, reports were presented, and Monroe was chosen as the site as the next meeting place. Everyone was at pains not to appear too confrontational lest Long and the General Assembly strike at the association again.

U. A. Bell delivered a calm, carefully worded presidential address that hardly mentioned the SBL. He concluded by saying that his speech was made "without ill will and with all friendliness; as an enemy of wrong and not of persons."[j] Walter J. Burke (1866–1941)[82] did a point by point takedown of the State Bar Act which demolished Hugh Wilkinson's claim that it was merely the Louisiana variant of the California statute.[k] J. Zach Spearing (1865–1942)[83] struck a more truculent chord when he surveyed the LSBA's current status and claimed a vital role for its future.

The SBL, he said, "was organized for the very purpose of supplanting this association. Everything that has been done before and after that State Bar was created by legislative act points to that very fact, that it was created to disintegrate us to destroy us-to destroy our usefulness-to destroy our place in the fraternity and in the public affairs of this State."[l]

Should the association submit? He answered "No, no, a thousand times no. I would rather be dead than say yes."

He believed his listeners agreed with him, but he recognized that both the association and the SBL competed for their loyal-

---

82 A New Iberian, Burke was a leading member of the LSBA. He was a state senator and a delegate to the Constitutional Conventions of 1898, 1913, and 1921. He drafted the state's first workman's compensation law. President of the Public Works Administration Advisory Board. See Jane B. Chaillot, "Walter James Burke," *Dictionary of Louisiana Biography Online*.

83 Spearing was LSBA president in 1921-22. Thereafter he continued as one of its prominent leaders until he died. As the quotation indicates, he was also a vehement anti-Black bigot. See Jane B. Chaillot, "James Zachary Spearing," *Dictionary of Louisiana Biography Online*.

ties. He exhorted them not to "consider the state bar as a competitor in our advance and our performance of our duties at the bar. It is not a competitor. Mind you, it has among its members every scalawag and pettifogger, every shyster lawyer, and, more than that, every negro lawyer in the State of Louisiana. Do you know and do you realize that you have been forced Into an association where every negro lawyer in the State of Louisiana is a member on the same footing, and with the same responsibility, rights, benefits, and privileges as you? Heavens alive, men, are we going to consider such an association as that a competitor? Let it go on and do what it will without the LSBA meddling in its affairs." Instead the association should stay together to become "missionaries and emissaries" who would enlarge it to wield an unprecedented influence throughout the state.

Two other presentations merit comment. One was a resolution that condemned an attempt by some legislators to impeach justices O'Niell, Odom, and Rogers and that commended them for their independence and courage in the face of "repeated public threats of impeachments and removal from office."[m] It passed with no dissent. However, apart from attracting the intended notice in the press, the resolution was meaningless because the move to punish the justices was dropped.The other was a talk by American Bar Association (ABA) President Scott M. Loftin, about a national bar program.[n] Warmly received, his remarks were less important than the fact of his presence. Off the record conversations with the Executive Committee provided firsthand knowledge of the LSBA's legal position, what could be done to preserve the organization, and how the ABA might help nationally. Loftin's presence was a visible sign of ABA support. That support was continued by his successors, each of whom attended all of the annual conferences after 1935. It was also an asset that prevented the ABA from acknowledging the SBL and representation in the ABA house of delegates.

Additional backing came from another national organization, the American Judicature Society. The editor of its publication informed readers about the State Bar Act and warned about its adverse political implications. Recognizing the LSBA as the state's official bar organization, he called upon the "decent" lawyers to continue making it "serviceable" and "improving its form at the earliest opportunity."[o] Liaisons with the American Law Institute (ALI) and the Association of American Law Schools (AALS) heightened national awareness too. Organized in the 1920s, the ALI advocated bettering social needs and the administration of justice by clarifying and simplifying federal and state laws. The institute encouraged scholarly legal research as well. The ALI was composed of chief justices, judges, deans, attorneys, and state bar association presidents, and a select LSBA committee linked the two organizations.[84] In 1938, the Louisiana State Law Institute (LSLI) was established by statute and housed on the Louisiana State University (LSU) campus with purposes that were duplicative of those of the ALI. An independent body, the LSLI advised the General Assembly on law reform, it afforded legislators guidance on statutory draftsmanship, and it conducted research on the civilian origins of state law. A year later, when Charles Vernon Porter announced LSLI's creation to the annual meeting, he noted that three LSBA members, John H. Tucker Jr., Monte M. Lemann, and Paul M. Hebert,[85] were the LSLI's first president, vice president, and secretary.[p]

Educational-minded attorneys and judges founded the Association of American Law Schools (AALS) in 1900. Member

84 The Louisianans who belonged initially were Chief Justice O'Niell; Judge and Tulane law Dean, Rufus E. Foster; LSU Dean R.L Tullis; Charles E. Dunbar Jr.; Monte M. Lemann; George H. Terriberry; and Edwin T. Merrick. See *Report of the Louisiana Bar Association*, 26 (1928):100, HeinOnline. They were all members of the LBA. Changes in membership after 1928, as well as who sat in the select committee, can be tracked in subsequent issues of the *Reports*.

85 Hebert (1907–1977) was dean of the LSU Law School from 1937 to 1977. After his death the law school was named for him.

institutions promoted legal education as an academic discipline and maintained faculties who were notable teachers and scholars. It was also intended as a learned society for professors and an institutional organization for member law schools and their deans. Professors at Tulane, LSU, and Loyola were inducted in 1909, 1924, and 1934. Their presence enhanced the prestige of their respective schools, and as their numbers grew, each school took on more of the academic characteristics that the AALS stood for. They were usually invited into the LSBA fold where they were important to the association's longstanding commitment to modernizing legal training and yet one more link to a highly powerful national legal society.[86]

The association made its presence felt nationally in other ways. At the annual meeting in 1937, the members not only came out against President Franklin D. Roosevelt's plan to enlarge the Supreme Court of the United States, but they required the Executive Committee to form a select committee to resist the proposal. Chaired by former resident Charles H. Dunbar Jr., and fitted with some of the association's biggest wigs, this committee consistently broadcast its objections to the public which brought them to the attention of relevant congressional authorities. According to Monte M. Lemann, the effort "played its part, along with the work on other similar Committees throughout the country, in bringing about the defeat of the proposal."[q87] During his presidency, Lemann named a special committee to collaborate with committees of an ABA section on ways to improve judicial administration.[88]

86 There is a brief history of the association on its website.

87 The other members were John D. Miller, Henry Plauché Dart Jr., Charles F. Fletchinger, Burt Henry, George H. Terriberry, Tulane law dean Paul W. Brosman, Eldon S. Lazarus, Joseph Merrick Jones, former resident Robert E. Bumbry, and M. Cary Thompson.

88 The other members were Charles F. Fletchinger, G. B. Barrett, George R. Blum, Cecil Morgan, former-Governor Luther E. Hall, E. L. Richardson, and Benjamin Wall Dart.

Another special committee participated in revising the rules of civil procedure for the federal district courts. Its chairman, former president John D. Miller, reported to the annual meeting in 1938 that their suggestions were considered and that several of them were adopted.[89] Then too, association leaders cooperated with the national commission that planned the sesquicentennial commemoration of the adoption of the Constitution.

Executive Committee and annual meetings were always given over to considerations about the state of the association. After 1935, many of these deliberations centered on improving the association's governance, the merits of two statewide bar organizations, relations with local bar associations, and bar integration. An integrated bar society was a statutory association to which every attorney must belong. The American Judicature Society (AJS) promoted integrated bars after World War I to encourage greater harmony among lawyers. Recognizing that erecting them required legislative action, the AJS drew up a model bill that it circulated across the nation and urged its adoption.[r] Walker B. Spencer warmed to the possibility; however, others were hostile because integrating the association meant accepting "undesirables," and that was a change too drastic. Whether to integrate came up after Long attacked the association in 1928. A special committee was appointed to study the matter but progress was so slow that it was disbanded. Nevertheless, bar integration would become a reality when the Longites launched the State Bar of Louisiana.[s]

Not least of these perennial considerations was concern for sustaining the LSBA financially. Memberships hit the pocketbooks. Paying dues to the LSBA, the SBL, and other local bar associations was difficult during the Great Depression. For

89 John D. Miller, "The Federal Rules of Civil Procedure," ibid., 146. Besides Miller, the members were Arthur O'Quin of Shreveport, M. Cary Thompson of Monroe, Paul G. Borron of Baton Rouge, and New Orleanians Eberhard P. Deutsch, René A. Viosca, Alfred J. Bonomo, and William C. Dufour, all of whom practiced routinely in the federal district court in the Crescent City, as did Miller.

most of the 1930s demands on income were greater than the membership dues brought in. Moving from Royal Street to 221 Baronne Street, the Canal Bank building, was so expensive that the 1935 annual report to the membership could not be printed, and to save money none were printed in later years.[t] As the costs associated with the librarian's salary, library upkeep, rent, supplies, travel, and annual meetings mounted, the Executive Committee borrowed against the value of the library collection and solicited loans or donations from members.

As part of its effort to increase income, the leadership fell back on an old standby, a standing committee, to recruit new members. There was a decline in numbers initially, but the committee's aggressive pursuit of recent law school graduates, young lawyers, and inactive attorneys yielded growth. Monte M. Lemann happily reported, in his presidential address, that as of 1938 the membership was the largest it had been in half a decade. The gain in the previous year alone had been the most ever for any single twelve months' period. He attributed that growth to the LSBA's attractiveness as a self-governing bar organization, but he also noted that the total membership still amounted to about only a third of all enrolled attorneys. Therefore he called for a redoubling of the effort to bring more of them into the fold, which would augment the income.[u]

Nevertheless, a year later the coffers were depleted, and to replenish them the Executive Committee took the difficult decision to sell its one remaining asset, the library. It advertised a collection of about twenty-five thousand volumes for fifteen thousand dollars. There was only one bid. It came from a Baton Rouge bookseller, Otto C. Claitor. The largest retailer of second-hand law books in the region, Claitor offered 8,265 dollars, or approximately thirty-three cents a volume.[v90] His offer dismayed

90 Claitor was foresighted enough to see a potential market for used law books as law firms shed outdated series of statutes, case reporters, and antiquarian volumes. He began the business in 1922 which made him one of the earliest vendors anywhere in the country. At the time of the sale,

the committee which had no choice but to accept the offer.[91]

While none of the foregoing activities were intended to eliminate the objectionable features of the State Bar Act, there were attempts to remove them. The first happened in April 1936. During the Monroe meeting the Executive Committee was instructed to confer with the SBL and local bar associations about proposing to the upcoming General Assembly changes that would make the statute more acceptable. Monte M. Lemann led a committee that conferred with representatives of the SBL and the New Orleans Bar Association. They suggested three amendments. One would restore the bar to its former independence. Another would empower only lawyers to elect members to the SBL Board of Governors. A third would return control of admissions and disbarments to the Supreme Court. The conference was a dud. Everyone agreed to a second sit-down that failed because the SBL representatives excused themselves for a lack of time. Nevertheless, a bill was introduced in the house of representatives that would have allowed lawyers to pick the Board of Governors and would have struck out the hated income disclosure mandate. These changes would come into force two years after the voters approved them. A letter from the Executive Committee to the house judiciary committee repeated the association's views without taking a position on the bill itself. Evidently, the bill's proponents gave it such a lukewarm endorsement that it was unfavorably reported

it was estimated that between 1847 and 1939 the LSBA had spent close to $60,000.00 developing the collection. See ibid., April 7,1939.

91 It was always an adventure to rummage in Claitor's warehouse. Because books were piled everywhere on the floor in no particular order or were crammed precariously in shelves that always seemed on the verge of collapse, one calculated one's searching with considerable caution. Several years before Claitor's burned in 2010, I asked if anyone had inventoried the LSBA library when it was purchased. I was told that if there had been an inventory it was long gone. Consequently, there is no extant record of a law library that was once among the oldest and largest in Louisiana.

out of the judiciary committee and defeated.[w]

The General Assembly was not in session until the spring of 1938. Ahead of that sitting, the Executive Committee tried again to have the Bar Act amended. Charles Vernon Porter recounted the attempt. He said that the association was "definitely, in no sense a political organization."[x] It had "no political fences to build, or axes to grind," nor did it "ever take part in the political campaigns in Louisiana." Its sole interest lay in quickly changing the SBL into a self-governing bar association free of legislative or gubernatorial intrusion. That stance was palpably evident when the Executive Committee held out an "olive branch with definite assurances on our part that this Association would consider its own corporate dissolution as soon as the Act was properly amended, which offer, it was thought, was complete evidence that we were not playing politics or seeking any unfair advantage for ourselves." People in Governor Leche's administration prepared the amendment, and there were promises that it would be enacted. Then, without any warning, the bill was killed. It died, Porter hinted gloomily, because "certain political leaders" wanted the Bar Act to stay unchanged).

But for the Louisiana Scandals of 1939 and 1940, the act probably would have remained unchanged into the foreseeable future. The scandals were a stunning consequence of Huey Long's assassination. He was barely cold in his mausoleum before his lieutenants hustled to become the next king fish but none of them was Long's equal nor could anyone garner the support of the others to replace him. The jostling played into the contentious gubernatorial election of 1936 that was won by Richard W. Leche[y] and Huey's brother Earl K. Long.[z] Leche was a man with a taste for the high life who supposedly remarked on becoming governor "When I took the oath of office, I didn't take any vows of poverty."[aa] That relaxed attitude typified his administration's tolerance of graft and corruption that more nearly resembled Reconstruction politics than at any other time in state history.

At first, the voters disregarded the mischief which seemed not all that different from the past. Then too, they inclined to look aside because they approved of Leche's alliance with the Roosevelt administration and its policies that redounded to their benefit. As 1939 began the enormity of the corruption started coming to light in stories that were appearing in the New Orleans *States*. Leche brushed them aside offhandedly saying the *States* was an opposition newspaper that was trying to discredit him. No one who should have attempted to investigate what was revealed. The filthy linen stayed in the dirty hamper until two reporters, Drew Pearson and Robert S. Allen, hung it out in their nationally syndicated column "The Washington-Merry-Go Round" that appeared in *The Washington Post* on June 17, 1939. A bold headline shouted the "Justice Department has evidence of WPA corruption in Louisiana: witnesses testify to work done on private estate of Governor Leche; say Federal supplies were diverted, hidden from WPA inspector." The story itself was based on information Pearson and Allen obtained in sworn affidavits from workers who had taken Works Progress Administration materials to build one of Leche's houses in Covington. That was shocking news to Louisiana readers because Leche was stealing from a federal program that was intended for their relief. A week later there was another startling, more infuriating exposure. LSU president James Monroe Smith had squandered millions of university dollars speculating on the stock market, and dozens of leading members in Leche's administration had robbed the university too. Leche resigned on June 26.[bb]

These and other revelations prompted a series of federal and state investigations. Leche and Smith were in a group of some 150 individuals and 40 organizations and businesses who were indicted, tried, and convicted between July 1939 and November 1940. The charges against them ranged from conspiracy to defraud, to income tax evasion, mail fraud, kickbacks, violations of antitrust laws, and theft of WPA labor and materials. Leche and Smith were among those who went to prison.[cc]

Earl Long announced his bid for reelection in September 1939. His announcement polarized the voters and the politicians. On one hand were those who remained loyal to the Longs. On the other was a bag full of angry plain citizens who wanted to cleanse the mess in Baton Rouge, newspaper reporters excited to square accounts with the Longs, old-line conservatives who wanted a return to the days before Long, and anti-Longs who saw a chance to rule Louisiana once more. Vincent Moseley, James H. Morrison, James A. Noe, and Sam H. Jones ran against Uncle Earl in the first primary.

SAM JONES from the Historic New Orleans Collection, 1980.160.

Jones was the least well known of the four, but his bona fides and political savvy propelled him to the governor's mansion. Born in 1897 in southwest Louisiana, he attended LSU but left to fight in World War I. Afterwards the voters of Beauregard Parish elected him to the 1921 constitutional convention, where he was its youngest delegate. Admitted to the bar in 1922, he practiced for a while in DeRidder before becoming an assistant district attorney in Calcasieu Parish and opening a law office in Lake Charles. He belonged to the LSBA and the American Legion, and he was a highly placed leader in both organizations. His record of public service was unspotted by connections with state politics, and that was his most appealing credential.[dd] Selling it became the ultimate theme in his campaign. Mindful that the Kingfish's legacy remained popular, even with his followers, Jones avoided criticizing Huey Long. Instead, he declared that "I am not running against a dead man. I am running against a gang of rascals as live as any gang that ever lived, and, I'm running to clean out every one of them."[ee] With the support of the LSBA and other reformers Jones came second to Earl Long in the first primary, but he narrowly defeated Long in the second primary and carried with him reform majorities in both houses of the General Assembly.

Jones's election portended the recreation of the LSBA. In March 1940 the Executive Committee unanimously adopted a resolution to repeal the State Bar Act of 1934 and to return supervision of the bar to the Supreme Court. The resolution was the handiwork of W. Pike Hall, Jr. A Shreveport attorney, Hall (1900–1949) was an LSBA officer throughout the 1930s He was the last president of the LSBA as a voluntary organization and its first president as a statutory association. His proximity to Governor Jones and Chief Justice O'Niell led to his chairing the committee that drafted the LSBA charter of 1941.[92]

Hall's resolution was approved at the annual meeting in April 1940. So was a bill he drafted that proposed a new state bar act. Copies of both were forwarded to Governor Jones and the appropriate committees in the General Assembly.[ff] On inauguration day Jones met with Hall, who had probably done more than anyone else to convince him to run for governor

92 Hall has no biographer but see "Pike Hall, One of State's Leading Lawyers Dies, *Shreveport Times*, 16 Dec. 1949, 1-2.

and who had worked tirelessly for his election. "Pike," he said, "there is one thing I want to see happen in Louisiana while I am governor. The bar of this State wants a self-governing, integrated bar. You fellows go to it, and I am behind you 100 percent all the way."[gg] True to his word, Jones included repealing the State Bar Act of 1934 and passing the integrated bar bill on his list of indispensable legislation.

Jones's floor leaders in the senate introduced both bills, and they were swiftly enacted. The integrated bar act was a carbon copy of the draft bill the LSBA had sent to the General Assembly. Its first section memorialized the Supreme Court "to create an association to be known as the Louisiana State Bar Association, which association shall be self-governing and may be organized as a corporation upon complying with the general corporation laws of this state." Section 2 required all attorneys to join a new LSBA and prohibited those who refused from practicing law in the state. The third section requested the Supreme Court to use its "inherent powers" to organize the new LSBA by regulating bar admissions, members' conduct, membership dues, and providing rules for punishing miscreant members.[hh] Section IV allowed the Supreme Court to confer subpoena power on the new association's officers and committees as an aid in all disciplinary matters. A fifth section commanded the Supreme Court to publish these rules in the *Louisiana Reports* and other suitable outlets. The next section stated that the invalidation of any part of the act did not render the remainder unconstitutional, and the final clause voided all prior legislation.

The repeal statute contained two sections. Section I merely declared that "Act X of the Second Extraordinary Session of 1934, as amended by Act XXI of the Third Extraordinary Session of 1934, is hereby repealed."[ii] The second section dissolved the SBL. Additionally, it commanded the state treasurer to hold all SBL assets until the new bar association was organized whereupon he was to turn them over to the new LSBA.

Governor Jones initialed both statutes into law respectively on July 9 and July 10, 1940. Three weeks later the SBL board of governors met in President Hugh Wilkinson's office in New Orleans to comply with the repeal statute. They ordered their assistant secretary to close the books and accounts, and then they dissolved the SBL. The last entry in its minute book is Mabel L. Perret's notation that she had delivered the assets to the state treasurer "as will more fully appear from a copy of [the] letter of transmittal in the file."[jj]

Meanwhile, Pike Hall and the justices were discussing how to implement the new bar act, and in August they agreed on a procedure. On or before the fifteenth of October 1940, the justices were supposed to name an advisory committee consisting of fifteen unpaid attorneys who would hold their meetings in New Orleans. Of the fifteen, one was elected from each of the eight congressional districts; the other seven were the president of the voluntary LSBA (Pike Hall), the deans of the Tulane, LSU, and Loyola law schools, the president of the Louisiana Law Institute, a member of the LSBA junior bar, and a lawyer chosen by Governor Jones, but if someone failed or refused to serve then the Supreme Court would pick a replacement. On October 17,1940; the justices announced their choices and swore in the committee.[kk]

Chaired by Pike Hall, the advisory committee was charged to propose a charter of incorporation and rules of governance for the statutory LSBA that the Supreme Court could accept with or without amendments. According to Hall the members "met many, many times in New Orleans" before they hammered out a draft.[ll] Separating into study groups, they spiritedly debated the charter's contents. For guidance they looked to the voluntary association's archives, its charters, the ABA constitution, its publications, and charters from other states as points of departure. Their reports went to an intermediary supervisory group, chaired by Hall, who rationalized them and sent them back for more deliberations. After the study groups finished this second go-round, the supervisory group made more changes and gave everything to Hall to draft the charter. His draft went through several iterations before the full advisory reviewed it again, approved it, and promptly handed it up to the Supreme Court. The justices promulgated it in mid-February 1941.

Spread across nearly twenty-five printed pages of text, the charter comprised fourteen articles. Articles one through three, the shortest, domiciled the new association in New Orleans and kept its name, purpose, and duration; the other eleven covered nearly everything else in exquisitely painstaking detail.[mm]

The first of the longer articles related to attorneys. A self-governing organization, the new association consisted of an integrated state-wide bar that eliminated all distinctions between lawyers and judges. Every lawyer, irrespective of social standing or legal training, was automatically enrolled. So were all licensed judges, although they were prohibited from practicing or becoming association officers so long as they were on the bench. Members were supposed to register within thirty days after having received a registration card. Those who failed to comply ceased being members, and their names were forwarded to the Supreme Court so they could no longer practice, but they could be reinstated if and when they signed up. According to a scale based on length of membership everyone, except sitting judges, paid annual dues. Delinquent dues-payers were liable to suspension within thirty days of being officially informed of their default, and they were certified to the Supreme Court as ineligible to practice. If they paid current and back dues, plus a fine then they could practice again.[nn]

Far more comprehensive articles affected the persons who managed the association's business, their duties, and the manner of their selection. Instead of a president, a secretary-treasurer, and a vice president for each of the seven supreme court districts, the charter established just three officers: president, secretary-treasurer, and vice president. The executive committee was no more. In its place was the board of governors that met every ninety days or at the president's call.

There were no more standing committees because matters that had come within their purview were outdated or they were folded into other articles. Fiscal affairs were more closely reckoned with as were the making or changing the association's by-laws. Officers were unpaid. They served one-year terms and were ineligible for re-election. Governors were also uncompensated, and they served staggered one- or two-year terms. With the exception of the officers, who were ex officio, the board of governors was drawn from the congressional districts, the law schools, the council of the Louisiana State Law Institute, the junior bar, and one person at large.

Candidates for both positions were nominated by nominating committees that were chosen by an open but intricate process of polling the membership. Elections were the responsibility of the secretary treasurer who conducted them according to a highly controlled system of mail-in ballots and a tightly prescribed schedule. The ballots had to be circulated and returned to the secretary treasurer well in advance of an annual meeting. Members might also propose someone by petition or from the floor but those nominations were strictly controlled. There were also detailed means to contest election results or to challenge the validity of someone's right to vote. As soon as the secretary treasurer counted the returns and verified them they were certified, and he published the results at the annual meeting.[oo]

The twelfth article laid down the standards for admissions to the bar and the Association's role in their implementation. Annually the board of governors named a committee of nine examiners to test law school graduates or applicants who had studied under an attorney's tutelage. The examiners wrote and administered two written tests a year, and their questions, or question, varied from one year to the next. An advisory committee of faculty from the law schools helped the examiners as needed, but it's more important part followed the tests. Within sixty days after an exam, the advisors reviewed the exam, the pass/fail results, and anything that affected the outcome or could be an improvement. Their written findings were given to the examiners, the board of governors, and to the justices. Candidates who passed were certified to the Supreme Court ahead of their introduction to the justices who swore them in, and they were licensed. A candidate who failed could be reexamined until he succeeded or quit trying. Licensed attorneys from other states could be admitted in Louisiana, assuming their credentials met the state standards.[pp]

Two of the final three articles dealt with discipline and standards of ethical behavior. Article XIII established a committee to investigate complaints against any member of the Association for professional misconduct or violations of law. Its five members were appointed annually by the Supreme Court at the recommendation of the board of governors. If the committee determined there was a violation but it was not serious enough to warrant suspension or disbarment, then it merely reprimanded an offender privately in writing. On the other hand, if the committee found serious violations, it prosecuted offenders on behalf of the association in the Supreme Court. Depending on the justices' decision, the result could be a suspension or disbarment.[qq] The standards that guided the committee were in the canon of ethics that constituted Article XIV. Hall's source was the then-current ABA canon. The charter's longest article, its forty-five canons ranged from "The Duty of the Lawyer to the courts" to "Aiding the Unauthorized Practice of Law." According to the provisions in Article XV, the charter could be amended by a secret vote of the membership but with one exception. Only the board of governors was authorized to alter the admissions and discipline articles, and then only if the Supreme Court approved their changes.[rr]

When Hall conferred with the justices on Valentine's Day, he pointed out the need for interim officers to serve until the first convention of the new association elected its officers. They decreed that the first convention would be held in

Lake Charles on April 18 and 19, 1941. In a separate order they named Hall and the advisory committee members interim officers of the association.[ss]

The meeting dates, the convention venue, and the attendees were the same for the old and new associations; Hall presided over both. Early on the morning of the eighteenth, Hall gaveled the voluntary association into a brief session. First up, the secretary-treasurer and standing committee chairmen presented their annual reports that were approved and recorded. Then Shreveport attorney W.W. Phillips was recognized. Phillips offered a resolution to disband the association and to pick liquidators to transfer the assets to the new one. After Hall opened the floor to discussion no one spoke against Phillips's motion. He called for the yeas and nays. Hearing no dissenting voices, he declared the voluntary association dissolved and adjourned its forty-fourth and final annual conference *sine die*.[tt]

A little while later, the delegates convened as the statutory association. Copies of its charter were in their chairs which was the first chance many of them had to read it. Hall called the session to order, and it began with an invocation by the pastor of Trinity Baptist Church, Lake Charles. His prayer was followed by greetings from the Lake Charles mayor, the local bar association, and a response from the Association. When Hall recognized all the attending state and federal judges, he said he thought that one of the finest things about the integrated LSBA was its possibilities for friendship and interchanges of ideas that would come from having lawyers and judges as active members of the same organization He went on to note that an illness kept Chief Justice O'Niell at home but that Justice Wynne Rogers would speak for the Supreme Court. Rogers, who hated public speaking, was succinct. He praised the voluntary association as having been a force for good, but he said the new one was even better because its embrace of all lawyers invested it with greater benefit to the bar and the people of Louisiana. Therefore, he concluded, at "this time I am happy to congratulate you on the part of our court and to wish you a happy and prosperous future."[uu]

Rogers's remarks were followed by Hall's presidential address. Because most of the audience was seeing the charter for the first time, Hall focused on how it had been prepared. He and his colleagues on the advisory committee had "threshed out and threshed out and discussed and cussed" the charter's composition. They were not always hopeful of success but in the end, they achieved what Hall described as a "workable and intelligible and understandable" charter that the Court had proclaimed.[vv] He praised everyone for their "assiduous labor.". Far from being "yes-men" they talked the sticky parts "over time and time again." "I just have this thought to impart to you," he continued, "there [was] no pride of authorship in this charter. It is what we [thought would] be a workable plan. We [knew] it [was] not perfection. We [knew] there [would] be imperfections in it. However, we [had] this enjoyable thought, that if something [was] in there that [was] not right, the lawyers of the State [could] change it by a simple majority vote." Indeed, he pointed out, time was allotted in the afternoon session for members to discuss the charter and to ask him questions. In closing, Hall thanked his listeners for their attentiveness and their great interest in the new association, but he also challenged them. Because the world was at war it was vital for lawyers everywhere to keep the processes of government functioning and to maintain liberty and democracy in America. Therefore everyone in the audience must do all "the ordinary daily tasks" of building up the association.[93]

There were two presentations during the afternoon session. The most anticipated of the two was Governor Jones's

93 Hall's address was followed by the secretary-treasurer's report and a talk about bar integration by Angus Gilchrist Wynne, a founder and first president of the Texas State Bar Association which began in 1940. Hall, presidential address, Report of the Louisiana State Bar Association , 19-28.

speech. Hall's brief introduction was more a reflection on a personal relationship than a long-winded presentation that endlessly glorified the governor. Jones was his friend, and for twenty years the two of them had toiled together at the bar and in the bar association, veterans' organizations, and civic societies. "I am proud of that friendship, I am proud of his record as a citizen, . . . and I am proud of him and grateful to him as the governor of the State of Louisiana."[ww]

Jones replied in kind and went on to say "It is a particular pleasure for me to be here to address the first convention of the new Louisiana State Bar Association. Today marks the beginning of a new and hope-filled future for the members of the bar of our State. It marks, officially, the end of an order that was unsought and undesired, and, in its place, the establishment of an organization integrating all of the members of the legal profession in Louisiana toward the advancement of the science of jurisprudence, the promotion of the administration of justice, and of the general welfare of the profession, and, finally, toward the encouragement of cordial intercourse among its members. The sword may now be sheathed. My pleasure," he continued, "comes not only from these facts as such, but also from the realization that the initial action toward the establishment of an integrated bar for Louisiana, directed and controlled by its members, was taken at the legislative session of 1940. This session, itself, will long be remembered by those whose blood rebels at despotism, whose spirit is imbued with the priceless significance of freedom. Freedom–not only from every form and shade of oppression, but freedom which suffuses the inner consciousness with an expanding tumult of creative energy–that which made and is, America. That I can so genuinely rejoice at having participated in this rebirth of a finer way of life in Louisiana I know will be forgiven me." Then he devoted the bulk of the speech to a long recap of the reform laws he pushed through the General Assembly. Concluding, he circled back to his opening theme, saying "Through the tumult and the chaos has come a finer Louisiana State Bar Association. May it be dedicated to the preservation of our new liberties, to the jealous guardianship of the integrity and honor of our state and of its people."[xx]

James Thomas Connor gave the second speech that was probably a pre-arranged response to Hall's challenge, considering its subject. On leave as Loyola's law dean, Connor was a commissioned officer in the federal Judge Advocate General's Department who was attached to the selective service office in New Orleans as legal adviser to the civilian draft board and to the draftees. It did not take him long to realize that the draft caused three issues that neither the War Department, the Judge Advocate General's Department, nor Congress had specifically contemplated when the Selective Services Act was adopted: How to protect the clientele of drafted attorneys, how to defend the legal rights of ordinary inductees, and how to safeguard the legal interests of inductee families. In Louisiana, those were matters for the LSBA to resolve, and there was no time to waste.[yy]

Connor's speech was well met with extended applause. As the clapping subsided, Hall opened the floor for a discussion of the charter, telling the delegates, "Don't be bashful."[zz] Nobody was. For an hour and a half he fielded questions, answered complaints, and ruled on amendments that were voted up or down. He adjourned the session as evening approached, and everyone went to the banquet.

Mid-morning on the nineteenth the delegates reconvened for their second session. An address by Jacob M. Lashly, president of the American Bar Association, preceded the introduction of resolutions. One acknowledged Lashly and the other speakers for their talks. Another invited the ABA to hold one of its future annual meetings in New Orleans. A third petitioned for the appointment of a state-wide legal aid committee to help military personnel and their families. Others were the usual ones that thanked everyone who had a hand in bringing off a successful conference. Electing new officers and a nominating committee was the last item of business. Hall called for nominations from the floor. Dan Deballion was elected president by acclamation as were the other officers and the nominating committee. With that, the first annual convention of the Louisiana State Bar Association was history.[aaa94]

94 Charles Payne Fenner reported the rechartering to the ABA. See "Bar Association News," *American Bar Association Journal*, 27 (1941): 464-65. His report also included a photograph of Daballion.

NOTES

a. $_{\text{WB}}$William Ivy Hair, *The Kingfish and His Realm: The Life and Times of Huey P. Long* (Baton Rouge, 1991), 298-327; $_{\text{WB}}$Bennett H. Wall et al., *Louisiana: A History*, 4th ed., (Wheeling, 2002), 311-19.

b. "Amendment to Rules," in La. Ann. 180 (1935): ix-xiv.

c. *The Times-Picayune* (New Orleans, La.), January 3, 1935: 10.

d. "Wilkinson's Address," in *Reports of the State Bar of Louisiana for 1934–1935* (Baton Rouge?, 1935), 1: 159-76, HeinOnline.

e. "Program," in *Reports of the State Bar of Louisiana for 1934–1935* (Baton Rouge?, 1935), 1: 6-7, HeinOnline.

f. *Reports of the State Bar of Louisiana for 1934–1935* (Baton Rouge?, 1935), 1: 158, HeinOnline.

g. "Official Election Returns," in La. Ann. of the Secretary of State (1936, 1938): 16-18, 33-37.

h. Paul Brosman, "A Neglected Duty," *Tulane Law Review*, 14 (1939–1940): 428-29.

i. "Resolution of W. Pike Hall Jr.," in "Executive Committee Minute Book" (January 5, 1935): 389.

j. U.A. Bell, "Presidential Address," in *Reports of the Louisiana State Bar Association, 1935–1941* (New Orleans, 1942): 6-10, HeinOnline.

k. Burke, "The State Bar of Louisiana," in *Reports of the Louisiana State Bar Association*, 16-26.

l. Spearing, "The Louisiana State Bar Association—Its Past, Its Present, Its Future," in *Reports of the Louisiana State Bar*, 10-16.

m. John R. Hunter, "Resolution," in *Reports of the Louisiana State Bar*, 45.

n. Lofton, "The National Bar Program," in *Reports of the Louisiana State Bar*, 39-45.

o. "Statutory Organization for Louisiana Bar: Legislature Adopts Act Intended to Deal with the Profession on a Political Basis," *Journal of the American Judicature Society*, 18 (1934-35): 110-11.

p. "An Act Designating the Louisiana State Law Institute, domiciled at the Louisiana State University Law School, as an official advisory law revision commission and legal research agency for the State of Louisiana

. . .," La. act. 168 in Acts of La. (1939): 429-33, HeinOnline; Frederick K. Beutel, "Trends in Modern Legal Education," ; Porter, "Presidential Address," in *Report of the Louisiana State Bar Association* (1939): 124-25; 1, 76, HeinOnline.

q. *Reports of the Louisiana State Bar Association*, 87, HeinOnline.

r. "Redeeming a Profession: Introducing a Practical and Logical Plan for Bar Organization Which Will Enable the Bar to Realize its Highest Ideals," *Journal of the American Judicature Society*, 2 (1918): 105-11.

s. Executive Committee "Minutes," (1934–1937): 369.

t. *Reports of the Louisiana State Bar Association*, 1, HeinOnline. As a cost saving measure, this single volume did not include the annual financial statements.

u. Monte Lemann, "Presidential Address," in *Reports of the Louisiana State Bar Association*, 140-41, HeinOnline.

v. "Obituary," *The Morning Advocate* (Baton Rouge, La.), June 4, 1975.

w. Robert E. Brumby, "Presidential Address," (April 23, 1937) in *Reports of the Louisiana State Bar Association, 1937*, 88-89, HeinOnline.

x. Charles Vernon Porter, "Presidential Address," (April 21, 1939), in *Reports of the Louisiana State Bar Association, 1937*, 177, 178.

y. Carl A. Brasseux, A New Orleanian, Leche (1898–1965) was a Long operative and Gov. Allen's legal adviser. "Richard Webster Leche," *Dictionary of Louisiana Online*: Louisiana Historical Association.

z. Morgan D. Peoples, "Earl Kemp Long," *Dictionary of Louisiana Online*: Louisiana Historical Association; Michael L. Kurtz and Morgan D. Peoples, *Earl K. Long and the Saga of Louisiana Politics* (Baton Rouge, 1990).

aa. Wall, *Louisiana: A History*, 314.

bb. Kurtz and Peoples, *Earl K. Long*, 92-102.

cc. Edwin A. Davis, *Louisiana: A Narrative History*, 3rd ed. (Baton Rouge, 1971), 343.

dd. W. Pike Hall Jr., "Introduction of Gov. Jones," (April 18, 1941) in *Report of the Louisiana State Bar Association for 1941* (New Orleans, 1942): 29-30, HeinOnline; Arthur W. Bergeron, "Sam Huston Jones, 1897–1978," *Dictionary of Louisiana Biography Online*: Louisiana Historical Association.

ee. Kurtz and Peoples, *Earl K. Long*, 105.

ff. "Resolutions," in *Reports of the Louisiana State Bar Association, 1934-1941*, 244-46, HeinOnline.

gg. *Report of the Louisiana State Bar Association for 1941*, 29.

hh. "An Act to Memorialize the Supreme Court to Create the Louisiana State Bar Association . . .," La. act. LIV in Acts of La. (1940): 363-66, HeinOnline.

ii. "An Act To repeal Act 10 of the Second Extraordinary Session of the Legislature of 1934, as amended by Act 21 of the Third Extraordinary Session of the Legislature of 1934 . . .," La. act. 55 in Acts of La. (1940): 366, HeinOnline.

jj. "Minute Book," (December 27, 1934-July 31, 1940). N. P. Perret's letter is missing.

kk. "Order of the Court," (August 22, 1940) in *Report of the Louisiana State Bar Association for 1941*, 93-94: "Order of the Court Appointing the Advisory Committee," (October 17, 1940) in *Report of the Louisiana State Bar Association for 1941*, 96.

ll. "Order of the Court Promulgating the Statutory Louisiana State Bar Association," (February 14, 1941) in *Report of the Louisiana State Bar Association for 1941*, 97.

mm. "Charter of 1941," in in *Report of the Louisiana State Bar Association for 1941*, 102.

nn. "Charter of 1941," in in *Report of the Louisiana State Bar Association for 1941*, 102-103.

oo. "Charter of 1941," in in *Report of the Louisiana State Bar Association for 1941*, 104-108.

pp. "Charter of 1941," in in *Report of the Louisiana State Bar Association for 1941*, 110-14.

qq."Charter of 1941," in in *Report of the Louisiana State Bar Association for 1941*, 114-17.

rr. "Charter of 1941," in in *Report of the Louisiana State Bar Association for 1941*, 102.117-26.

ss. "Memorandum to the justices," (February 14, 1941) in *Report of the Louisiana State Bar Association for 1941*, 96-97; "Order of the Court Appointing Interim Officers of the Statutory Louisiana State Bar Association," (February 14, 1941) in *Report of the Louisiana State Bar Association for 1941*, 97.

tt. "Essential Excerpts from Stenographer's Transcript," (April 18, 1941) in *Reports of the Louisiana State Bar Association, 1934-1941*, 250-52, 252-55, HeinOnline; "Resolution to Disband the Voluntary Louisiana State Bar Association," (April 18, 1941) in *Reports of the Louisiana State Bar Association, 1934-1941*, 250-51.

uu. *Report of the Louisiana State Bar Association for 1941*, 2-4.

vv. Pike Hall, "Presidential Address to the statutory Louisiana State Bar Association," (April 18, 1941) in in *Reports of the Louisiana State Bar Association, 1934-1941*, 4-19.

ww. "Hall's Introduction," in *Reports of the Louisiana State Bar Association, 1934-1941*, 29.

xx. " Gov. Jones's Address," (April 18, 1941) in *Reports of the Louisiana State Bar Association, 1934-1941*, 130-45.

yy. James Thomas Connor, "Organizing the Bar for National Defense," (April 18, 1941) in *Reports of the Louisiana State Bar Association, 1934-1941*, 41-45.

zz. *Reports of the Louisiana State Bar Association, 1934-1941*, 45-63.

aaa. *Reports of the Louisiana State Bar Association, 1934-1941*, 63-90.

Epilogue

Birthing the new Louisiana State Bar Association (LSBA) from 1940 to 1941 was its latest incarnation. Its parentage arose in the territorial and early statehood years when judges had joined with New Orleans lawyers to fashion appellate court rules of practice and processes for supervising the bar. In time their relationship had inspired the connection between the Supreme Court of Louisiana and an elite congregation of attorneys that had spawned the direct ancestor of the LSBA, the New Orleans Law Association (NOLA). Chartered as a self-governing voluntary society, it had tightened the ties with the Supreme Court while it had sought to enhance the reputation of Crescent City attorneys. It had remained a small, low-key group that eschewed electoral politics as an organization, although its members were often prominent political figures. The NOLA had survived the Civil War and Reconstruction, but only just. It drew staunchly anti-Black segregationists who supported control of state government by a Whites-only Democratic Party. Nevertheless, it had come near to dissolution until it was re-chartered as the voluntary state-wide Louisiana Bar Association(LBA). It was linked to the American Bar Association (ABA) and other national legal societies. The word "state" was inserted when it renamed itself as part of its effort to stave off Huey P. Long. Long's minions enacted the State Bar of Louisiana (SBL) and limited the LSBA's ties with the Supreme Court. Then came the events that ended with the new statutory association.

The new charter reconfigured the association's structure and solidified its relationship with the Supreme Court. It decreed who belonged, the requirements for admission, standards of behavior, and the consequences for failure to abide by an extensively articulated canons of ethics. All were issues that were controversial from the Louisiana Purchase down to and including the debates about defining the new association itself. Consequently, the charter divided a forever line between old versus new; ancient versus modern.

The promises of this charter were paper ones. What happened next was not like changing a light bulb, throwing a switch, and voila all was changed for the better. Far from it. In the spring of 1941, whether the bench, bar, legislature, and people accepted its reforms was no certainty. Because of the State Bar Act, there was damage to repair. Long's followers had to be wooed into believing that the new association was not only for the benefit of corporate clients, it would look after their interests too. Country lawyers who had been excluded from the voluntary society had to be convinced of their acceptance. The discontent of those who had opposed integrating the bar had to be dispelled. Determining the places of women and African American attorneys was problematic. Deciding what to do with the lawyers and judges who had corrupted themselves in the scandals of 1939 was an open question. There were much needed changes to criminal law, the statutes, and the codes that were still unaddressed. And how would the Association adjust to a Whites-only Democratic Party that was still suffused with Longism?

These were issues for the presidents and board of governors to reconcile. None of them could possibly have anticipated how America's entry into World War II would abruptly and irrevocably change them, and as they adapted, the spirit of reform retreated to the margins. The history of their adjustments to the modern Louisiana State Bar Association since April 1941 is a tale yet to be told, but there was where its early history ended.

Bibliographic Essay

Records of the New Orleans Law Association are all but nonexistent. The singular exception is the founding documents that were reprinted in the 1899–1900 annual report of the Louisiana Bar Association. That report and later ones contain minutes, membership rolls, lists of officers, committees and committee members, financial accounts, presidential addresses, lectures, member activities, and relations with the courts and the General Assembly. Digital texts are accessible through the HathiTrust electronic archive or HeinOnline digital archive.

The Earl K. Long Library at the University of New Orleans houses the historic archives of the Supreme Court of Louisiana, a collection that spans the years between 1813 and 1921. The contents consist of minute books, docket books, opinion books, and case files. Generally, these records are well preserved for the Orleans Supreme Court District but most of the archives for the western district are lost. The Orleans records are available online via the DSpace Repository. Some cases and other materials for the years 1920 to 1940 are archived at the Louisiana State Archives in Baton Rouge, Louisiana. Records after 1935 are housed at the Supreme Court in New Orleans.

Texts of state constitutions and relevant acts of the General Assembly, its proceedings, and cases argued before the Supreme Court are accessible through the HeinOnline digital archive.

The early rules of court regarding legal education and the bar are gathered in Warren M. Billings, ed., *The Historic Rules of the Supreme Court of Louisiana, 1813–1879* (Lafayette, La., 1985).

Housed at the bar association offices on Saint Charles Avenue in New Orleans are some remaining items for the period before 1941. A run of minute books begins in 1908 extends to the 1940s, and there is a collection of annual reports that began in 1899. The minute book kept by the State Bar of Louisiana survives; it covers the entirety of that organization's brief existence. Another item pulls back the curtain on legal education after the Civil War. A group of lawyers founded an alumni association in 1869. They were former students of elderly members of New Orleans Law Association, some of whom had been teachers in the University of Louisiana Law Department, which preceded the Tulane University School of Law. The sole surviving record of the association is a minute book that begins in 1869 and ends in 1887. Among the contents are the constitutions and bylaws and the members' names. The New Orleans Law Association is identified as the meeting venue, which suggests it provided classrooms too. Eventually, the group may have been absorbed into the Tulane University School of Law.

Private papers have not survived in abundance. Consequently, newspapers are a source for personal details about the individuals who appear through this book. The Library of Congress' online Chronicling America Collection, Louisiana State University's Digitizing Louisiana Newspaper Project, and News Bank aggregate pertinent newspapers. Biographical information can also be gleaned from electronic aggregations such as the Louisiana Biography and Obituary Index, Louisiana State Archives Vital Records Search, the New Orleans Public Library Louisiana Division City Archives and Special Collections and Find A Grave. On the other hand, there are biographical sketches of more recognizable members of the Association who were public officeholders or sat on the bench. See Glenn R. Conrad et al., eds., *A Dictionary of Louisiana Biography*, 3 vols. (Lafayette, La., 1988, 1998), or its online version; Joseph G. Dawson III *The Louisiana Governors: From Iberville to Edwards* (Baton Rouge, 1990); Janice K. Shull, *The Chief Justices of Louisiana: Life Sketches* (New Orleans, 2007).

Not to be overlooked are books that shaped Louisiana law and practice. These are identified and discussed by Billings in *The Historic Rules of the Supreme Court*; "A Course of Legal Studies: Books That Shaped Louisiana Law" in Warren M. Billings and Mark F. Fernandez, eds., *A Law Unto Itself? Essays in the New Louisiana History*; and "A Neglected Treatise: Lewis Kerr's *Exposition* and the Making of Criminal Law in Louisiana" in the 1997 issue of *Louisiana History*. Book historian Dr. Florence M. Jumonville's essay '"Formerly the Property of a Lawyer–"Books That Shaped Louisiana Law" in the 2009 issue of *Tulane European & Civil Law Forum* made a significant addition to the discussion. Not to be overlooked are two University of New Orleans master's theses: Robert F. Karachuk's, "A Workman's Tools: The Law Library of Henry Adams Bullard" and Rosemarie Davis Plasse's "Tools of the Profession: New Orleans Attorneys and Their Libraries From Statehood to Secession (1813 to 1861)".

Books, articles, dissertations, theses, and other secondary literature are identified throughout the footnotes and need not be rehearsed here.

BIBLIOGRAPHY

Adams, William H., "Christian Roselius," *Dictionary of Louisiana Biography Online*: Louisiana Historical Association.

Acts of Louisiana.

"Affidavit of Thomas A. Edwards," (September 19, 1934) in Porter v. Conway case file (No. 33147).

"Alleged Klan Members Found Guilty," *Madera Mercury* (Madera, Ca.) November, 6, 1923.

"An Act Designating the Louisiana State Law Institute, domiciled at the Louisiana State University Law School, as an official advisory law revision commission and legal research agency for the State of Louisiana . . .," La. act. 168 in Acts of La. (1939): 429-33, HeinOnline

"An Act Erecting Louisiana into Two Territories, and Providing for the Temporary Government Therof," US Congress, *U.S. Statutes at Large 6th through 12th Congress*, 2 (1799-1813): 283-290, Library of Congress

"An Act to amend and re-enact Sections 8, 11 and 12 of Act N. 10 of the Second Extra Session of the Legislature of 1934," La. act. XXI in Acts of La. (1934): 135-37, HeinOnline.

"An Act to create a public corporation to be known as "The State Bar of Louisiana" . . .," La. act. X in Acts of La. (1934): 70-75, HeinOnline.

"An Act to amend Sections 6 and 10 of Act No. 96 of 1904 . . .," La. act. CLXXIX in Acts of La. (1904): 369-70, HeinOnline.

"An Act to amend Sections 16 and 30 of Act No. 97 of the Acts of the Legislature of the year 1922," La. act. 215 in Acts of La. (1924): 397, HeinOnline.

"An Act to increase the number of judges of the Supreme Court of the State of Louisiana," in *Acts of Louisiana, 1839*: 4, HeinOnline.

"An Act to Memorialize the Supreme Court to Create the Louisiana State Bar Association . . .," La. act. LIV in Acts of La. (1940): 363-66, HeinOnline.

"An Act relative to applicants for a license to practice law," La. §. in *Acts of Louisiana, 1822*: 72, HeinOnline.

"An Act to Organize the Supreme Court of the State of Louisiana, and to Establish Courts of Inferior Jurisdiction," La. § 17-18 in *Acts of Louisiana, 1813*: 28, HeinOnline.

"An Act to Promote the Comfort of Passengers on Railway Trains . . . and to Repeal All Laws and Parts of Laws Contrary to or Inconsistent with the Provisions of this Act," La. In *Acts of Louisiana, 1890*: 152-54, HeinOnline.

"An Act to provide for calling, holding, conducting and regulating primary elections . . .," La. act. 97 in Acts of La. (1922): 178, 201, HeinOnline.

"An Act to Provide for the Calling of a Convention for the Purpose of Readopting, Amending, or Changing the Constitution of the State" La. in *Acts of Louisiana, 1844*, 31-32, HeinOnline.

"An Act to provide for the acquisition for, and or the construction and maintenance of a courthouse building in the City of New Orleans . . .," La. 96 in Acts of La. (1904).

"An Act to provide for the construction and maintenance of a courthouse building in New Orleans . . .," La. act. LXXIX in Acts of La. (1902): 106-10.

"An Act to repeal Act 10 of the Second Extraordinary Session of the Legislature of 1934, as amended by Act 21 of the Third Extraordinary Session of the Legislature of 1934 . . .," La. act. 55 in Acts of La. (1940).

"Article VII," in La. Ann. (1916).

"Article XXIX," in La. Ann. (1916).

Baldwin, Simeon E., "Founding of the American Bar Association," *American Bar Association Journal*, 3, (1917).

Bar Association, "Minute Book."

Bauer, Carl A., "Henry Adams Bullard," *Dictionary of Louisiana Biography Online*: Louisiana Historical Association; Dora J. Bauer "The Career of Henry Adams Bullard." *Louisiana Historical Quarterly*, 23, (1940).

Bell, U. A., "Presidential Address," in *Reports of the Louisiana State Bar Association, 1935–1941* (New Orleans, 1942)

Bergeron, Arthur W., "Sam Huston Jones, 1897–1978," *Dictionary of Louisiana Biography Online*: Louisiana Historical Association.

Beutel, Frederick K., "Trends in Modern Legal Education," ; Porter, "Presidential Address," in *Report of the Louisiana State Bar Association* (1939).

Billings, Warren M., "A Neglected Treatise: Lewis Kerr's *Exposition* and the Making of Criminal Law in Louisiana." *Louisiana History: The Journal of the Louisiana Historical Association*, 36, (1997).

Billings, Warren M., "From This Seed: The Constitution of 1812" in $_{\text{WB}}$*In Search of Fundamental Law: Louisiana's Constitutions, 1812-1974*, ed. Warren M. Billings and Edward F. Haas (Lafayette, 1993).

Billings, Warren M., *Historic Rules of the Supreme Court of Louisiana, 1813-1879* (Lafayette,1985).

Billings, Warren M., , "Mixed Jurisdictions and Convergence, The Louisiana Example," in *Magistrates and Pioneers: Essays in the History of American Law*, ed. Warren M. Billings, (Clark, 2011).

Boudreaux, Sybil Ann, "The First Minute Book of the Supreme Court of the State of Louisiana, 1813 to May 1818: An Annotated Edition" (master's thesis, University of New Orleans, 1983).

Brasseux, Carl A., "Richard Webster Leche," *Dictionary of Louisiana Online*: Louisiana Historical Association.

Brasseux, Carl A., "Wynne Gray Rogers," *Dictionary of Louisiana Biography Online*: Louisiana Historical Association.

"Brief of Attorney General Porterie," (September 25, 1934) in Porter v. Conway case file.

Brosman, Paul, "A Neglected Duty," *Tulane Law Review*, 14 (1939–1940).

Brumby, Robert E., "Presidential Address," (April 23, 1937) in *Reports of the Louisiana State Bar Association, 1937*.

Bullard, Henry Adams and Curry, Thomas, *A New Digest of the Statute Laws of the State of Louisiana From the Change of Government to the Year 1841* (New Orleans, 1842).

Bullard, Henry Adams, *A Discourse on the Life and Character of the Hon. François Martin*.

Burke, "The State Bar of Louisiana," in *Reports of the Louisiana State Bar Association.*

"By-Laws," in *Proceedings of the Louisiana State Bar Association*: 17; "Charter of 1899," in *Proceedings of the Louisiana State Bar Association*: 23.

Canon, E. A., "On the Necessity of a Court of Criminal Appeals," *The Louisiana Law Journal*, 1, no. 2 (1841).

Carriere Jr., Marcus, "Thomas Jenkins Semmes," *Dictionary of Louisiana Biography Online*: Louisiana Historical Association.

Chaillot, "Étienne Mazureau," *Dictionary of Louisiana Biography Online*: Louisiana Historical Society.

Chambers, Henry E., *A History of Louisiana Wilderness–Colony–Province–Territory–State–People*, 3 (Chicago and New York, 1923).

"Charter of 1899," in *Proceedings of the Louisiana State Bar Association, 1899* (New Orleans, 1899).

"Charter of 1941," in in *Report of the Louisiana State Bar Association for 1941.*

Chiorazzi, Michael G., "François-Xavier Martin: Printer, Lawyer, Jurist," *Law Library Journal*, 80 (1988): 63-99; Judith Schafer, "Martin, François-Xavier (1764-1846), jurist and author," *American National Biography Online.*

"Committee Report, Final Draft of Articles Relative to Legislative Procedure," In Appendix A of La. Ann. (1916).

"Committee Report, Tentative Draft of Articles Relative to Judiciary System," In Appendix B of La. Ann. (1916).

"Complaint of Burt W. Henry, Esmond Phelps, J. Zach Spearing, Charles F. Dunbar Jr., Charles F. Fletchinger, Edwin T. Merrick Jr., Blanc Monroe, and Monte M. Lemann," (October 19, 1934) in Executive Committee Minute Book (June 2, 1934–June 1937).

"Concurrent Resolution of the General Assembly of Louisiana," in *The Complete Works of Edward Livingston on Criminal Jurisprudence . . .*, Edward Livingston, (New York, 1873), 4.

Connor, James Thomas, "Organizing the Bar for National Defense," (April 18, 1941) in *Reports of the Louisiana State Bar Association, 1934-1941.*

Conrad, Glen R., "Charles Erasmus Fenner," *Dictionary of Louisiana Biography Online*: Louisiana Historical Association.

Conrad, Glen R., "Gaston Louis Porterie (1885–1953)," *Dictionary of Louisiana Biography Online*: Louisiana Historical Association.

"Constitution of the State of State of Louisiana Adopted in Convention at the City of New Orleans, May 12, 1898."

"Contract with A. B. Stanard," Louisiana Digital Library: (March 1, 1907).

Courthouse Commission, "Minute Book," Louisiana Digital Library (October 17, 1902).

Courthouse Commission, "Minute Book," (April 2, 1906).

Courthouse Commission "Minute Book," (April 3, 1906).

Cox, Isaac Joslin, "General Wilkinson and his Later Intrigues with the Spaniards," *The American Historical Review*, 19, no.4 (1914).

Craft, John H., "The Law Department of the University of Louisiana and Tulane University: Predecessor of the School of Law of Tulane University," unpublished paper, 1978, Tulane School of Law Archives, New Orleans, La.

Cunningham, George E., "Constitutional Disenfranchisement of the Negro in Louisiana, 1898." *Negro History Bulletin*, 29 (1966).

Dargo, George, "Derbigny, Pierre Auguste Charles Bourguignon, (1767-1829)," *American National Biography.*

Dart, Henry Plauché, "Address at the Corner-Stone Ceremonies" (New Orleans, 1908): Louisiana Digital Library

Dart, Henry Plauché, "Presidential Address," (May 12, 1899) in *Report of the Louisiana State Bar Association.*

Dart, Henry Plauché, "The History of the Supreme Court of Louisiana," in *Louisiana Reports* (1913).

Davis, Edwin A., *Louisiana: A Narrative History*, 3rd ed. (Baton Rouge, 1971).

Deacon, William M., *Reference Biography of Louisiana Bench and Bar, 1922* (New Orleans, 1922).

De Conde, "Edward Livingston (1764–1836) lawyer and politician," *American National Biography Online* (2000).

De Latte, Carolyn E., "Carleton Hunt," *American National Biography Online.*

Douglas, Jeannine E., "Steamboats and Slaves: Issues and Liabilities in Louisiana, 1831-1861" (master's thesis, University of New Orleans, 1991).

Downs, Solomon W., "Notes on Criminal Law," *The Louisiana Law Journal*,1, no.3 (1842).

Dugas, Kathy T., "An Immigrant's Journey to Wealth and Power: The Story of François-Xavier Martin," *Louisiana History: The Journal of the Louisiana Historical Association*, 50, no.3 (2009).

"Essential Excerpts from Stenographer's Transcript," (April 18, 1941) in *Reports of the Louisiana State Bar Association, 1934-1941.*

Executive Committee "Minutes," (1934–1937).

Fernandez, Mark F., *From Chaos to Continuity: The Evolution of Louisiana's Judicial System, 1712–1862*, 1st ed. (Baton Rouge, 2001).

Find a Grave: "Alfred Hennen."

Folch, Vicente and White, David Hart, *Governor in Spanish Florida*, 1787-1811 (University Press of America, 1981).

"Fournet's Notice," (September 21, 1934) in Porter v. Conway case file.

"Fournet to Frugé," (September 21, 1934) in Porter v. Conway case file.

Gaspard, Elizabeth, "The Rise of the Louisiana Bar: The Early Period, 1813–1839," *Louisiana History: The Journal of the Louisiana Historical Association*, 28, no.2 (1987).

Gentry, Judith Fenner, , "Pierre August Bourgignon Derbigny," *Dictionary of Louisiana Biography Online*: Louisiana Historical Society.

Goetsch, Charles C., "Simeon Eben Baldwin (05 February 1840–30 January 1927)," *American National Biography Online*.

" Gov. Jones's Address," (April 18, 1941) in *Reports of the Louisiana State Bar Association, 1934-1941*.

Green, George D., *Finance and Economic Development in the Old South: Louisiana Banking, 1804-1861* (Redwood City, 1972).

Hair, William Ivy, *The Kingfish and His Realm: The Life and Times of Huey P. Long* (Baton Rouge, 1991).

"Hall's Introduction," in *Reports of the Louisiana State Bar Association, 1934-1941*.

Hall Jr., W. Pike, "Introduction of Gov. Jones," (April 18, 1941) in *Report of the Louisiana State Bar Association for 1941* (New Orleans, 1942).

Hall Jr., W. Pike, "Hall's Introduction," in *Reports of the Louisiana State Bar Association, 1934-1941.*

Hall Jr., W. Pike, "Presidential Address to the statutory Louisiana State Bar Association," (April 18, 1941) in in *Reports of the Louisiana State Bar Association, 1934-1941.*

Hass, Edward F., *Political Leadership in a Southern City: New Orleans in the Progressive Era* (Ruston, 1988).

"Hardy [sic] F. Brunot Succumbs at 83," *The Times-Picayune* (New Orleans, La.), March 12, 1944.

Hart, W. O., *Report of the Commission on Uniform State Laws in Louisiana for 1914* (Baton Rouge, 1914).

Hart, William O., "Women's Rights in Louisiana," *Louisiana Historical Quarterly*, 4 (1921).

Hatcher, William B., *Edward Livingston: Jeffersonian Centurion in the American Southwest* (Baton Rouge, 1940).

Helis, Thomas W., "Of Generals and Jurists, The Judicial System Under Union Occupation, May 1862–April 1865," in *A Law Unto Itself*, Billings and Fernandez.

Hémard, Ned, "A New York Hill," in *New Orleans Nostalgia: Remembering New Orleans History, Culture and Traditions* (New Orleans , 2013).

Hewitt, Lawrence L., "David Glasgow Farragut (05 July 1801–11 August 1870)," *American National Biography Online.*

Higginbotham, Jay, "Pierre Soulé," *Dictionary of Louisiana Biography Online*: Louisiana Historical Association.

Hollander, John, *American Poetry: The Nineteenth Century* (New York, 1939).

Hunter, G. Howard, "Fall of New Orleans and Federal Occupation," 64 Parishes Encyclopedia Online.

Hunter, John R., "Resolution," in *Reports of the Louisiana State Bar.*

Hyde, et al. v. Jenkins, La. Rep 192 (La. 1834).

Ingram, Alton Earl, "The Twentieth Century Ku Klux Klan in Morehouse Parish Louisiana" (master's thesis, Louisiana State University, 1961).

Jackson, Joy J. "Joseph Adolphus Rozier," *Dictionary of Louisiana Biography Online*: Louisiana Historical Association.

"John St. Paul, 72, Former Justice Expires at Home," *The Times-Picayune* (New Orleans, La.), November 6, 1939.

"Joint Resolution of the Senate and House of Representatives," (January 30, 1835) in Acts of La.

Journal of the Convention Called for the Purpose of Re-Adopting, Amending or Changing the Constitution of the State of Louisiana (New Orleans, 1845).

"Judgment of Judge W. Carruth Jones," (September 24,1934).

"Judge Overton Final Rites Held at Lake Charles," *The Times-Picayune* (New Orleans, La.), September 11, 1934: 1.

"Justice Overton Dies Suddenly on Eve of Election," *State-Times Advocate* (Baton Rouge, La.), September 10, 1934: 1.

"Justice St. Paul Retired Because Health Declined," *The Times-Picayune* (New Orleans, La.), May 1, 1934.

Kruttschnitt, Ernest B. speech, (February 8, 1898) in *Official Journal of the Proceedings of the Constitutional Convention of the State of Louisiana* (New Orleans, 1898).

Kurtz, Michael L. and Peoples, Morgan D., *Earl K. Long and the Saga of Louisiana Politics* (Baton Rouge, 1990).

Labbé, Ronald M., "That the Reign of Robbery Will Never Return to Louisiana: The Constitution of 1879," in *In Search of Fundamental Law*, 81-93.

Lanza, Michael L. "Little More Than a Family Meeting, The Constitution of 1898."

Laverty v. Duplessis, 3 Mart. (O.S.) 52, La. 1813.

Lemann, Monte, "Presidential Address," in *Reports of the Louisiana State Bar Association.*

Leovy, Sidney J., "The Ante-Bellum Bench and Bar."

Lombardi, Tara, "Designing a Courthouse: The Winning Architects." *De Novo*, 8 (2010).

Long, Huey P., speech, (April 14, 1928).

Louisiana Supreme Court, "Minute Book," Historical Archives of the Supreme Court, 4.

Louisiana Supreme Court, "Minute Book," Historical Archives of the Supreme Court, 9.

Martin, François-Xavier, *Reports of Cases Argued and Determined in the Supreme Court of Louisiana, 1809–1830* (New Orleans, 1846–1851).

Martin, François-Xavier, *The History of Louisiana* from *the Earliest Period*, 2 (New Orleans, 1827-1829).

Maxeiner, James R., "David Dudley Field (13 February 1805–1894)," *American National Biography Online.*

McCloskey, Bernard, "The New Orleans Courthouse."

McGovern, Charles, *Sold American: Consumption and Citizenship, 1890–1945.*

"Membership Roster," in *Proceedings of the Louisiana State Bar Association, 1898–1902*, (New Orleans, 1870), 1.

"Memorandum to the justices," (February 14, 1941) in *Report of the Louisiana State Bar Association for 1941.*

Merrick, Edwin T., *Revised Civil Code of the State of Louisiana* (New Orleans, 1900).

Milner, P. M., speech, (May 7, 1915).

"Minute Book," (December 27, 1934-July 31, 1940).

Morgan, Cecil B., "Constitution of Form of Government of the State of Louisiana" in *The First Constitution of the State of Louisiana*, (New Orleans, 1975).

Morse, Isaac Edward, "Observations on the Present Judiciary System in the Western Districts of the State of Louisiana," *The Louisiana Law Journal*,1, no. 4 (1842).

Morse, Isaac Edward, , "Report of the Attorney General, 1854," HathiTrust (1841).

"Motion of L. L. Perrault," (September 28, 1934).

"Notice of Intention to Run."

Nystrom, Justin A., "White League," 64 Parishes Encyclopedia Online.

"Obituary," *The Morning Advocate* (Baton Rouge, La.), June 4, 1975.

Official Journal of the Proceedings of the Constitutional Convention of the State of Louisiana Begun and Held in the City of Baton Rouge March 1, 1921.

Ogden v. Blackman, La. 1813, 304 (La. 1814).

"O'Niell's Dissent."

"Order appointing Higgins," (September 17, 1934).

"Order for the appearance of E.A. Conway," (September 20, 1934).

"Order for the appearance of J. Cleveland Frugé et al," (September 20, 1934).

"Order of the Court Appointing the Advisory Committee," (October 17, 1940) in *Report of the Louisiana State Bar Association for 1941*

"Order of the Court Appointing Interim Officers of the Statutory Louisiana State Bar Association," (February 14, 1941) in *Report of the Louisiana State Bar Association for 1941.*

"Order of the Court," (August 22, 1940) in *Report of the Louisiana State Bar Association for 1941*

"Order of the Court Promulgating the Statutory Louisiana State Bar Association," (February 14, 1941) in *Report of the Louisiana State Bar Association for 1941.*

"Our Judges: The Supreme Court of Louisiana," *The Times Picayune* (New Orleans, La.), May 1, 1887: 10.

Peoples, Morgan D. "Earl Kemp Long," *Dictionary of Louisiana Online*: Louisiana Historical Association.

"Petition of Thomas F. Porter Jr.," (September 20, 1934).

Plauché, Vance, "Short Sketch of the Fourteenth Judicial District Over Fifty Years Ago, 1920–1925," *Louisiana History: The Journal of the Louisiana Historical Association*, 18 (1977).

"Porterie's Notice," (September 24, 1934).

"Porterie Petitions to the Court."

"Porterie's President's Address," (January 31, 1935).

Pritchett, Carla Downer, "Case Law Reporting in Nineteenth-Century Louisiana," in *A Law Unto Itself?: Essay in the New Louisiana Legal History*, ed. Warren M. Billings and Mark F. Fernandez (Baton Rouge, 2001).

"Presidential Address," (May 6, 1905).

"Presidential Address" (May 7, 1915).

Proceedings of the Louisiana State Bar Association.

"Proclamation, May 1, 1862" in *The War of the Rebellion: A compilation of the Official Records of the Union and Confederate Armies,* comp. Robert N. Scott, et al. (Washington, D.C., 1880-1901), 1, no. 6

Report of the Commission to Revise the Civil Code of Louisiana to Jared Y. Sanders Governor of Louisiana (Baton Rouge, 1910), 23

Report of the Louisiana State Bar Association.

"Resolution to Disband the Voluntary Louisiana State Bar Association."

"Resolution of the Executive Committee," (July 3, 1934).

Richard Henry Wilde to John Walker Wilde (February 4, 1844) in Edward L. Tucker, ed., "Henry Wilde in New Orleans: Selected Letters, 1844–1847," *Louisiana History: The Journal of the Louisiana Historical Association*, 7 (1966)

Rivet, Charles G., "Commercial Evolution in the Catahoula Basin with Perspectives on Two Frontier Families" (master's thesis, University of New Orleans, 1997).

Robinson, Merritt M., *A Digest of the Penal Law of the State of Louisiana, Alphabetically Arranged* (New Orleans, 1841).

Robinson, Merritt M., *Louisiana Reports* (New Orleans, 1847).

Rodriguez, Junius P., "Claiborne, William Charles Coles (1775-1817)," *American National Biography* (2001).

"Scandal in the Court: The Rise and Fall of Judge Rice Garland," *Southern Studies: An Interdisciplinary Journal of the South*, 24, (2017).

Schoenfeld, Mrs. Robert, "Jean (John) Baptiste Fournet," *Dictionary of Louisiana Biography Online*: Louisiana Historical Association.

Schott, Matthew J., "Huey Long: Progressive Backlash?" *Louisiana History: The Journal of the Louisiana Historical Association*, 27 (1986).

Shepherd Jr., Samuel C., "In Pursuit of Louisiana Progressives," *Louisiana History*, 46 (2005).

Shull, Janice, *The Chief Justices of Louisiana: Life Sketches* (New Orleans, 2007).

"Speech to the State Bar of Louisiana," (January 31, 1935).

"Spencer's Resolution."

State v. Judge of the Commercial Court, 15 La. Rep. (La. 1840).

"Summary of Events." *American Law Review*, 5 (1871).

"Territorial Acts of Louisiana, 1805," La.: 105, 414-64, HeinOnline.

The Convention of '98. A Complete Work on the Greatest Political Event in Louisiana's Political History, And a Sketch of the Men Who Composed It, Hathi Trust (New Orleans, 1898).

"The Klan in Morehouse," *The New York Times*.

The Lake Charles American Press.

The Times-Democrat (New Orleans, La.).

The Times-Picayune (New Orleans, La.).

Tregle Jr., Joseph, "The Governors of Louisiana: Pierre Auguste Charles Bourguinon Derbigny 1828-1829." *Louisiana History: The Journal of the Louisiana Historical Association*, 22, no.3, (1981).

Trefoousse, Hans L., "Benjamin Franklin Butler (05 November 1818–11 January 1893)," *American National Biography Online.*

Tucker, John H., "Source Books of Louisiana Law," *Tulane Law Review*, 6, no. 2.

"Veteran Justice of the High Tribunal Taken by Death," *The Times-Picayune* (New Orleans, La.), April 19, 1941: 1.

Vincent, Charles, "Black Constitution Makers: The Constitution of 1868," in *In Search of Fundamental Law*, 69-80.

Wall, Bennett H., *Louisiana, A History*, 4th ed. (Wheeling, 2002).

Wegmann, Mary Ann, "Jackson's Bodyguards, Lawyers Who Fought in the Battle of New Orleans," Law Library of Louisiana Online: accessed February 21, 2021.

"Wilde, Richard Henry," *Biographical Directory of the United States Congress, 1774–Online.*

Williams, T. Harry, *Huey Long* (New York, 1969).

Windell, Marie, "Edward Livingston," *Dictionary of Louisiana Biography Online*: Louisiana Historical Society."

"Winston Overton, Justice of High Court, Dies," *The Times-Picayune* (New Orleans, La.), September 10, 1934

Marie, Windell, , "Henry Plauché Dart," *Dictionary of Louisiana Biography Online*: Louisiana Historical Association.

Wilson, James D., "Archibald Thomas Higgins," *Dictionary of Louisiana Biography Online*: Louisiana Historical Association.

Wilson, James D., ""Felix Pierre Poché," *Dictionary of Louisiana Biography Online*: Louisiana Historical Association.

Young, Sheridan E., "Louisiana's Court of Errors and Appeals, 1843–1846," in Billings and Fernandez, *A Law Unto Itself.*

Appendix A

Presidents of the Louisiana State Bar Association, 1847-1941

New Orleans Law Association

John Randolph Grymes, 1847–1848
Alfred Hennen, 1848–?
Christian Roselius ?–?
Edward Rawle ?–?
E.A. Bradford ?–?
James McConnell ?–?
Henry Plauché Dart, 1898–1899

Louisiana Bar Association

Henry Plauché Dart, 1898–1901
Bernard McCloskey, 1901–1905
Edwin Thomas Merrick, 1905–1907
William S. Parkerson, 1907–1909
Edward Hughes Randolph of Shreveport, 1909–1911
Joseph W. Carroll, 1911–1913
Benjamin Wall Kernan, 1913–1915
Edward T. Weeks, 1915–1917
George H. Terriberry, 1917–1918
Charles A. McCoy of Lake Charles, 1918–1919
Walter L. Gleason, 1919–1920
Albin Provosty, 1920–1921

J. Zachary Spearing, 1921–1922
Fred G. Hudson, Jr. of Monroe, 1922–1923
William W. Westerfield, 1923–1924
Ventress Jones Smith of New Iberia, 1925–1926
Esmond Phelps, 1926–1927
Sidney L. Herold of Shreveport, 1927–1928
Benjamin F. White of Alexandria, 1928–1929

LOUISIANA STATE BAR ASSOCIATION

Charles F. Fletchinger, 1929–1930
Charles Cecil Bird Jr., of Baton Rouge, 1930–1931
Charles E. Dunbar Jr., 1931–1932
Joseph D. Barksdale of Shreveport, 1932–1933
Henry D. McCall, 1933–1934
U.A. Bell of Lake Charles, 1934–1935
John D. Miller, 1935–1936
Robert B. Bumbry, 1936–1937
Monte M. Lemann, 1937–1938
Charles Vernon Porter of Baton Rouge,1939–1939
Eugene Stanley, 1939–1940
W. Pike Hall Jr. of Shreveport, 1940–1941

Appendix B

Annual Meeting Sites, 1898-1941

1898: New Orleans, Louisiana

1899: New Orleans, Louisiana

1900: New Orleans, Louisiana

1901: New Orleans, Louisiana

1902: New Orleans, Louisiana

1903: New Orleans, Louisiana

1904: New Orleans, Louisiana

1905: New Orleans, Louisiana

1906: New Orleans, Louisiana

1907: Shreveport, Louisiana

1908: New Orleans, Louisiana

1909: Alexandria, Louisiana

1910: Baton Rouge, Louisiana

1911: Lake Charles, Louisiana

1912: New Orleans, Louisiana

1913: New Orleans, Louisiana

1914: Gulfport, Mississippi and New Orleans, Louisiana

1915: New Iberia, Louisiana

1916: Opelousas, Louisiana

1917: New Orleans, Louisiana

1918: New Orleans, Louisiana

1919: Baton Rouge, Louisiana

1920: New Orleans, Louisiana

1921: Shreveport, Louisiana

1922: Monroe, Louisiana

1923: Alexandria, Louisiana

1924: New Orleans, Louisiana

1925: Baton Rouge, Louisiana

1926: Texarkana, Texas. Joint meeting with the Texas and Arkansas Bar Associations.

1927: New Orleans, Louisiana

1928: Shreveport, Louisiana

1929: Lafayette, Louisiana

1930: Monroe, Louisiana

1931: Baton Rouge, Louisiana

1932: New Orleans, Louisiana

1933: Shreveport, Louisiana

1934: Lake Charles, Louisiana

1935: Alexandria, Louisiana

1936: Monroe, Louisiana

1937: New Orleans, Louisiana

1938: Baton Rouge, Louisiana

1939: Alexandria, Louisiana

1940: Shreveport, Louisiana

1941: Lake Charles, Louisiana

APPENDIX C

CHARTERS OF THE LOUISIANA STATE BAR ASSOCIATION, 1847-1941

The charters of the Louisiana State Bar Association are available in *Reports of the Louisiana State Bar Association.* The charters from 1847, 1855, and 1899 are available online through HathiTrust under the title *Reports of the Louisiana Bar Association v.1/6 1898/1904.* Those charters are in the public domain. The charters from 1929 and 1941 are available in print under the title *Reports of the Louisiana Bar Association v.1/10 1941/1952* at various public libraries. Physical copies of the charters of 1929 and 1941 can be located using HathiTrust.

INDEX

ABOUT THE AUTHOR

Warren M. Billings, distinguished professor of history, emeritus at the University of New Orleans, is a student of colonial Virginia and Louisiana law. He graduated A. B. from the College of William & Mary, A.M. from the University of Pittsburgh, and PhD from Northern Illinois University. Widely published, his books include *The Historic Rules of the Supreme Court of Louisiana, 1813–1879* (Lafayette, La., 1985), *In Search of Fundamental Order: Louisiana's Constitutions, 1813–1974* [ed, with Edward F. Haas] (Lafayette, La., 1993), *A Law Unto Itself?: Essays in the New Louisiana Legal History* [ed. with Mark F. Fernandez] (Baton Rouge, La., 2001) *Magistrates and Pioneers: Essays in the History of American Law* (Clark, New Jersey, 2011), *The Supreme Court of Louisiana: A Bicentennial Sketch* (New Orleans, 2013), *A Unexpected Collector: The Making of An Historian's Law Library* (Austin, Texas, 2013). He has been Visiting Williams Professor of Law at the University of Richmond and Visiting Professor of Law at the College of William & Mary. In 1976, he negotiated the deposit of the historic archives of the Supreme Court of Louisiana in the Earl K. Long Library at the University of New Orleans. As the collection became accessible for research, he began a seminar that became foundational for the rise of the New Louisiana Legal History. The late Chief Justice John A. Dixon Jr. appointed him court historian in 1982, and he was renamed Bicentennial Historian of the Supreme Court of Louisiana in 2013. A past fellow of the American Bar Foundation and a former Virginia

Historical Society Mellon Research Fellow, he is an honorary life member of the British and Irish Association of Law Librarians and the Company of Fellows of the Louisiana Historical Association. The Louisiana Historical Association presented him its Garnie W. McGinty Lifetime Achievement Award, and the Virginia Museum of History and Culture conferred its Richard Slattern Award for Excellence in Virginia Biography upon him.